God and Me! 2

Ages 10-12

Linda Washington
& Jeanette Dall

For my sister, Gloria, who studies God's Word daily and teaches it to others.

~ JAD

For Sophia Rammell, and Mary and Rachel Lillyman, who liked the first one.

~ LMW

GOD AND ME!® 2 FOR AGES 10-12
©2014 by Linda Washington & Jeanette Dall, twentieth printing
ISBN10: 1-58411-056-2
ISBN13: 978-1-58411-056-9
RoseKidz® reorder #L46829
JUVENILE NONFICTION/Religion/Devotion & Prayer

RoseKidz®
An imprint of Rose Publishing, Inc.
17909 Adria Maru Lane
Carson, CA 90746
www.Rose-Publishing.com

Cover Illustrator: Phyllis Harris
Interior Illustrator: Aline Heiser

Printed in the United States of America

Table of Contents

Table of Contents

Table of Contents

Introduction

Do you enjoy seeing gardens with beautiful flowers and healthy vegetables? If you have ever helped care for a garden you know that it takes a lot of work to make it beautiful. The soil needs to be prepared and the seeds or plants put in the ground. Rain and sunshine make the plants sprout and grow. Weeds need to be chopped out. Sometimes you have to rid the garden of bugs and other critters. But once everything is growing and looking great, you can relax and enjoy the wonderful smells, sights and tastes of your garden.

Devotions with God are like growing a garden. First you must plan what to plant. Then you have to gather everything you need. Finally, you should calm your mind so you can hear what God has to say to you, which sometimes means getting rid of the "bugs" in your life at the time, such as TV or the Internet or whatever it is. The neat thing about spending time with God is you can enjoy the sunshine of His love and the rain of His blessings your whole life!

This book is filled with fun stories and activities to help you grow closer to God. You will read about people who may remind you of those in your own life–maybe even you! You'll see that with God's help you can face any situation.

You can read the devotionals in this book whenever you want and in whatever order you like. Each one has a topic and a Scripture. Try to memorize it! Then there is a story and some questions to answer. After your prayer, take a look at the activity. The projects and puzzles will help you act on what you've just learned. At the back of the book you will find answers to the puzzles (not that you'll need them!).

So get ready to grow in God's garden. It's the quietest, most beautiful place you can ever imagine. It's a place where you will never stop growing!

Loving God

Worshipful

I can worship God by acknowledging His holiness.

Worship the Lord in the splendor of his holiness.

~ 1 Chronicles 16:29

Like the Cherubim

Celine Taylor pointed to the picture of the cherubim in the Bible dictionary. "We were talking about these in Sunday school," she told her mother. "Do you think they look like this for real, Mama?"

Mrs. Taylor shrugged. "Honey, no one knows exactly what those angels looked like. The artist just had to draw something. What made you look that up anyway?"

Celine shrugged as she tugged on one of her braids. "We were talking about the story in Isaiah where he saw God in the temple. I was just wondering what cherubim looked like. Why do you think God would make something that can't look at Him?" She pointed to the wings covering the face of the cherubim.

Mrs. Taylor shrugged again. "Maybe they remind us that God is holy. When we worship Him, we think about who God is. He's above sin. His holiness inspires our worship."

Celine put her hands over her eyes.

"What are you doing?" her mother asked.

"I'm trying to imagine myself like the cherubim in front of God." She suddenly felt her mother's hand on her shoulder.

"Now that's the way to be worshipful!" her mother said.

Your Turn

1. Celine's mother mentioned that God is holy. What does that mean to you?

_____

_____

2. How does knowing that God is holy help you to worship Him?

_____

_____

Prayer

Lord God, You are holy. Remind me to worship You. Amen.

Worship Your Way

Worship isn't just something adults do. You can do it too. You can be like the psalm writers. Use the space below to write your words of praise to God for His holiness. Use words or pictures.

Worshipful

Worship isn't just an action; it's also an attitude.

I rejoiced with those who said to me, "Let us go to the house of the Lord."

~ Psalm 122:1

Attitude Is Everything

"Well, I'm glad that's over with," Leslie Harrington said, followed by a grin at her friend Jalise. She was surprised that Jalise did not immediately agree with her. They usually complained about church as they waited for their parents to pick them up after youth church. "Hello? Did you hear me?"

"I heard you." Jalise seemed quieter that day.

"What's with you?"

Jalise blushed. "I…um…kinda liked the service today."

Leslie stared at her. "Are you kidding me?"

"No…I just…like coming to church these days. It's like my dad said: 'Attitude is everything.' I, uh, asked God to help me want to worship Him."

Leslie didn't know what to say. She wanted to call Jalise a traitor, but she knew that wasn't right. As they waited in silence, Leslie thought about something her mother once said to her: "People who love God are glad to worship Him." She flipped a blond strand behind her ear as she cast a glance at Jalise. Jalise really looked glad. Three weeks ago she had acted as if she had to be dragged to church, kicking and screaming. Now…

Hmmph, Leslie thought, frowning. *I can't help it if I don't want to go to church sometimes.*

Your Turn

1. Why is a person's attitude important in worship?

_____

_____

2. What do you think it takes to have a worshipful attitude?

_____

_____

Prayer

Lord, help me to have a worshipful attitude. Amen.

Who's Worshipful?

Worshiping God doesn't always involve praise. It involves an attitude of the heart. Look up the Scripture for each person below. How worshipful is she or he? Shade in each "attitude meter" to rate where each person falls. Shading seven to 10 squares means a person is worshipful. One to three squares means the person is not really ready. Four to six squares means you're not sure. Then shade in an "attitude meter" for yourself!

Jezebel
1 Kings 18:4; 19:2

Not Ready   I'm Not Sure   Ready for Worship

David
2 Samuel 7:18

Not Ready   I'm Not Sure   Ready for Worship

Diotrephes
3 John 1:1-3, 1:9

Not Ready   I'm Not Sure   Ready for Worship

You

Not Ready   I'm Not Sure   Ready for Worship

Consistent

God never changes.

Jesus Christ is the same yesterday and today and forever.

~ Hebrews 13:8

Chameleon Kid

Brooke was upset by the way her friend Vanika behaved. She decided to discuss it with her older sister, Diane. "I never know how Vanika is going to act or what she is going to say," Brooke began. "When she's with the church group, she seems honest and sincere. But when she's around the kids at school, she makes fun of God and going to church. Why do you think she acts that way?"

"Vanika is a real chameleon kid," Diane answered.

Brooke looked confused. "Huh?"

"Time for a short biology lesson, little sis. A chameleon is a lizard that can change color according to its surroundings. It may be green, yellow or white one minute, and the next minute it may be brown or black. The temperature, light and lizard's feeling control these changes.

"Sometimes people are like chameleons," she continued. "They might say what people want to hear, or they laugh at things that really aren't funny just because everyone else is laughing."

"Oops. I think I might have some chameleon in me, too," Brooke said.

Diane nodded her head. "We're all a little 'lizardly' at times. But fortunately for us, God is never a chameleon. He doesn't love us one day and hate us the next. No matter what we do, God is consistent and doesn't change the way He feels about us. God always loves us and forgives us."

Your Turn

1. Think of some situations where you might behave like a chameleon. How can you change your behavior and stand up for what you believe?

_____

_____

2. Why is it important that God is always consistent?

_____

_____

Prayer

Lord, thank You for never changing how You feel about me. Help me be consistent in what I do and not act like a chameleon. Amen.

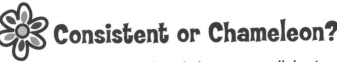

Consistent or Chameleon?

To be consistent means to act and speak the same way all the time–no matter what the situation may be. A consistent Christian always tries to act in a God-pleasing manner. How do you rate yourself? Are you a consistent Christian or are you part chameleon kid? Put a check in the box that tells how you act most of the time.

	Consistent Christian	So-so Kid	Chameleon
When I'm with church friends			
When I'm with my family			
When I'm with my school friends			
When I'm with someone who is making fun of God			
When I'm with someone who is being mean to another kid			
When I'm with strangers			
When I'm alone			
When I'm in a dangerous or scary situation			
When I'm with someone who doesn't know about God			
Most of the time			

Consistent

My actions need to go along with what I believe.

Create in me a pure heart, O God, and renew a steadfast spirit within me.

~ Psalm 51:10

Great Expectations

"This is impossible–totally out-of-the-question impossible," declared Kelly as she slammed shut her Bible study guide. "I'd have to be Jesus Himself to do this!"

"Whoa! Slow down, girl!" said her father. "What has you so stirred up?"

Kelly reopened her book and read Deuteronomy 8:1, "'Be careful to obey all the commands I am giving you today.' We're supposed to explain how we are going to do that. Like I said–it's impossible."

Mr. Bingham nodded. "You're right. We are sinners so we can't obey all of God's commandments. That's why Jesus died for us, to forgive our sins. But we need to be consistent in trying to obey, and we need to be consistent in asking Jesus for forgiveness when we disobey."

"Consistent–I don't understand exactly what that means," said Kelly.

"It means that your actions go along with what you believe. What you do tomorrow should be like what you did today. People around you will know what to expect of you and how you will react to certain situations."

"I think I get it," said Kelly. "Like I consistently get up late and have to rush to get ready for school?"

Mr. Bingham laughed. "Yes, you could say you're consistent in your time-challenged morning behavior!"

Your Turn

1. Think of one consistent behavior you have. Is it good or not-so-good?

_____

_____

2. Do you think it makes a difference to others if you are consistent in your actions and behavior? Why or why not?

_____

_____

Prayer

Dear God, thank You for Your consistent behavior. Help me to follow Your example. Amen.

Rainbow Cookies

Carefully following a recipe or directions makes the product turn out consistently the same. That's what will happen with these rainbow cookies. These cookies can also remind you and everyone who eats them that God is consistent and always keeps His promises.

What You Need

cookie dough (store-bought)
flour
food coloring
rolling pin
wax paper
cookie sheet

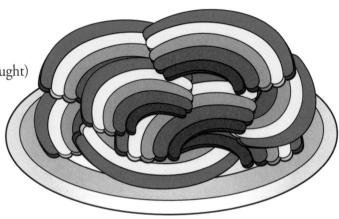

What to Do

1. Add a little flour to the dough so you can easily roll it out.

2. Divide the dough into five equal parts.

3. Add one or more different colors of food coloring to each part. For example, if you combine red and yellow, you get orange.

4. Roll each color of dough into strips ¼" thick. Cut the dough so each strip is about 4" long.

5. Stack the strips on top of each other, wrap them in wax paper and put them in the refrigerator overnight.

6. The next day, arrange the colored slices on a cookie sheet and curve them into a rainbow shape.

7. Ask an adult to help you bake the cookies at 375 degrees for 6 to 8 minutes.

Loyal

God wants me to be loyal to Him.

*O Lord…keep this desire in the hearts of your people forever,
and keep their hearts loyal to you.*

~ 1 Chronicles 29:18

Suppose

The fifth- and sixth-grade Sunday school class was playing its favorite game: "Suppose."

"Suppose your best friend wasn't a Christian and wanted you to do something wrong. Would you go along with your friend?" Mr. Conners, the teacher, asked.

"No way!" Matt said.

"Me neither," his cousin Michelle said softly.

"You would!" Matt hissed. "Remember what your friend Renae wanted you to do?"

Mr. Conners overheard them. "What's this?"

Michelle shot Matt a look. She didn't want to blab her life to everyone in the class. While she hesitated, Matt said, "Renae wanted her to ignore the new girl in their class and say nasty things about her."

"I didn't want to do it!" Michelle said. "But Renae said the girl didn't fit in because she dressed weird and talked with an accent."

Some of the other kids began talking at once. Mr. Connors called for quiet. "As we were saying earlier, God wants us to be loyal to Him. If you had to choose between staying loyal to Him and being loyal to a friend, which would you choose?"

Your Turn

1. How do you show loyalty to God?

_____

_____

2. Would God call you a loyal friend? Why or why not?

_____

_____

Prayer

Lord, I want to be a loyal friend to You. I need Your help. Amen.

20

Loyalty Poster

Make a poster for your bedroom wall to remind you to always be loyal to God. It can help you to remember that God comes first before friends.

What You Need

white poster board
ruler
stickers and other decorations

pencil
markers
reusable putty

What to Do

1. Use a pencil to print "Love + Obedience=Loyalty to God" in large block letters. Make it look like a math problem.

2. Fill in the letters with bright colors.

3. Decorate the poster with markers, stickers, glitter or anything else that you like.

4. Put your Loyalty Poster on your wall or the back of your door to remind you of true loyalty.

Loyal

God wants me to be loyal to my friends.

A friend is always loyal, and a brother is born to help in time of need.

~ Proverbs 17:17 NLT

The Swim Party

Jasmine and Gloria were doing their homework at Jasmine's house when Jasmine's brother, Kyle, stuck his head in the door. "Hey, Jas, a girl from your class called before you got home. Here's her name and number," he said as he tossed a paper on the table.

Jasmine and Gloria looked at the scribbled name: Megan Miller. "What do you think she wants?" asked Gloria.

"Guess we won't know unless I call," Jasmine said as she reached for the phone.

"I'm having a swim party for my birthday," Megan said. "It's on Saturday at 2. Can you come?"

Jasmine could hardly believe what she was hearing. Megan and her four friends always did everything together. They were the really "cool" girls in sixth grade. "Uh, I'll have to ask my mom," Jasmine stammered.

"Oh, one more thing," Megan went on. "I'm not inviting all the girls in our class. So don't tell Gloria about this, okay? Bye."

"What did she want?" Gloria asked.

What should I say? wondered Jasmine. *What am I going to do?*

Your Turn

1. If you were Jasmine, what would you do? What would you say to Gloria?

_____

_____

2. Can your friends count on your loyalty–no matter what?

_____

_____

Prayer

Lord, thank You for the friends You have given me. Help me to be loyal to them. Amen.

Loyalty Crossword

The Bible tells of many people who were loyal. Can you figure out who they are and fit their names into the crossword puzzle? The solution is on page 233.

Across

1. The only disciple at the cross (John 19:26)

2. He was loyal to God in a den of lions (Daniel 6:16)

4. Mary's loyal husband (Matthew 1:24)

6. He was loyal to God during a great flood (Genesis 7:5, 6)

7. She was loyal to her mother-in-law (Ruth 1:16)

Down

1. He was David's best friend (1 Samuel 20:42)

3. Abraham was loyal to this nephew (Genesis 12:4, 5)

4. Your best and most loyal Friend (John 15:13, 14)

5. The loyal apostle who wrote most of the New Testament (Romans 1:1)

Loyal

Christians are loyal to their beliefs.

Neither you nor anyone else can serve two masters. You will hate one and show loyalty to the other, or else the other way around—you will be enthusiastic about one and despise the other.

– Luke 16:13 TLB

The "Hot" Book

Boy did I luck out, thought Ashley. *No homework! I can read all night.* Soon she was settled into a corner of the couch with a bag of chips and the hottest book in sixth grade.

Ashley was so absorbed in her reading that she didn't even hear her mother come into the room. Mrs. Beacon said, "Hi, Ashley. What are you reading?"

Ashley was so startled that she jumped in surprise. "Wow, Mom, you scared me," she said as she recovered. Then she held up the book. "All the girls in my class are reading this book. Chloe loaned me hers for a few days."

Her mother took the book and read the description of the story on the back cover. Ashley had a funny feeling in her stomach as she watched her mother's face. "I read a review of this book, Ashley," she said. "I really don't think it's something you should read. It's about witches."

"Mom!" Ashley protested. "Everybody is reading it! I know it's not real–it's just a story. And anyway, I don't have any homework tonight."

"Even if it is a story, it can make you feel that non-Christian ways of living are okay. When that happens you're not being loyal to God or to your beliefs as a Christian."

Your Turn

1. Why is loyalty to God important?

_____

_____

2. Can you be loyal to two different beliefs? Why or why not?

_____

_____

Prayer

Dear God, help me to always be loyal to You and Your teachings. Amen.

Love in Action

Christians show their love to God through their actions. Circle the word that doesn't belong in each heart. Then write the words, in order, on the lines. You will discover the most important way to show love to God. The solution is on page 233.

blue
God
green
red

boat
car
wants
truck

us
horse
cat
dog

table
chair
couch
to

be
pen
pencil
marker

leaf
trunk
loyal
branch

daisy
to
tulip
rose

two
Him
three
six

and
star
moon
sun

piano
trumpet
flute
His

book.
magazine.
Word.
newspaper.

Repentant

Repentance is more than just saying I'm sorry; it involves action.

Repent, then, and turn to God, so that your sins may be wiped out.

~ Acts 3:19

A Theory of Repentance

"What's that thing?" Gena Barnett asked her sister, Lola, as she leaned over Lola's shoulder.

"An equation," Lola explained. "Pythagorean theorem. We have to learn it in geometry. You wouldn't understand."

Gena stared at it. "$A2 + B2 = C2$? You're right. I don't understand it." She flopped on a chair at the table. "Mom's really mad at me."

Lola glanced up. "You know why."

Gena shrugged. "I told her I was sorry I lied to her."

"Yeah, but you don't act sorry. For one thing, you keep lying. You know Mom hates lying."

"Who asked you?"

"You're the one who came to me."

Lola wrote a word on a piece of paper, then passed it to Gena.

"'Repentance,'" Gena read. "So what does that mean?"

"It means being sorry and acting like it. You like math, right?"

"Yeah, but not this geometry stuff."

"Here." Lola took the paper and wrote something, then passed it to Gena.

"'Thought + will = action,'" Gena read. "So?"

"So this adds up to repentance. You think, 'I don't want to lie to Mom anymore.' Then you decide, 'I won't lie to Mom anymore.' Then you don't do it!"

Gena looked at her older sister. "You think you're so smart...well, maybe I think that, too!"

Your Turn

1. When you're sorry about something, how do your actions show it?

_____

_____

2. Look at Lola's equation for repentance. How will you do that?

_____

_____

Prayer

Dear Jesus, help me to be sorry and mean it. Amen.

A Change of Heart

Many people in the Bible had a change of heart about sin. Find the names below in the puzzle. When you find "Paul," you'll also find a three-word message that goes diagonally from the A in his name. Write the message after the sentence below.

David   Judah   Job   Lost son
Lydia   Matthew   Paul   Peter
Sinners   Woman [at the] well   Zacchaeus

```
L Y D I A Q U E R T Z
L H I I H S A Z A C C
E L O H W U Z R I G H
W P J N A E Y L O H E
N E P O D A V I D Y M
A T H S B H B K O A T
M E L T X C A U V L L
O R E S T C C D J O Y
W O L O P A U L U K T
B X Q L N Z M V C J O
M H Y T S R E N N I S
Q M O L K P J B C E T
M O O N J U N E T U N
```

These people repented. _____.

The solution is on page 233.

Repentant

God helps me say, "I'm sorry," and mean it.

If we confess our sins, he is faithful and just and will forgive us our sins and purify us from all unrighteousness.

~ 1 John 1:9

Really Sorry

"Why doesn't Uncle Jerry believe in Jesus?" Trina Laurence asked as she watched her mother prepare dinner.

"Well," said her mother as she wiped her hands on a dish towel, "I think Uncle Jerry believes in God, but he doesn't want to follow God."

"Why not?"

"It's hard to explain. I don't think Uncle Jerry is really sorry for the bad things he's done. We've all done wrong things. God wants us to be sorry about those things and turn to Him."

"Maybe he's sorry and just doesn't know how to say he's sorry." Trina loved her uncle. She couldn't imagine that he'd ever done anything wrong. Yet she knew that he didn't go to church or read the Bible.

"God knows when we're really sorry or when we're just faking it," her mom said. "He wants us to be sorry for our sins and to want to do the right thing. Then He helps us."

"Maybe Uncle Jerry can ask God to help him be sorry."

"That's a good idea."

Your Turn

1. What did Uncle Jerry need to do?

_____

_____

2. Do you need to do what Uncle Jerry needs to do? If so, use the prayer below.

_____

_____

Prayer

Lord, I'm sorry for my sins. Thank You, God, for Your forgiveness. Amen.

28

Advice for the Sorry

Solve the rebus to find good advice for Uncle Jerry…and for you!

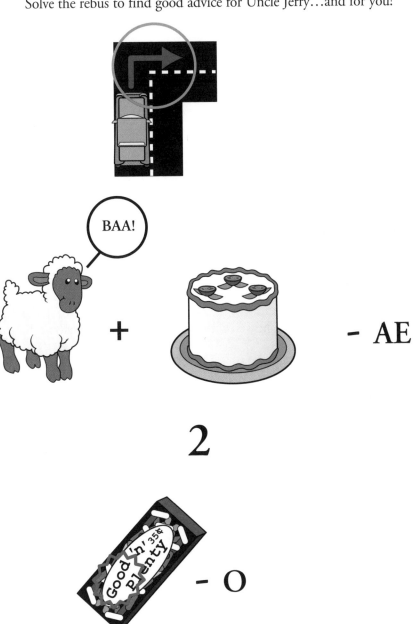

The solution is on page 233.

Thankful

I can give thanks to God for all He gives me.

Give thanks to the Lord, for he is good; his love endures forever.

~ Psalm 107:1

Happy Thanksgiving?

Thanksgiving was one of Molly's favorite holidays. All the McPherson uncles, aunts and cousins went to Grandpa and Grandma McPherson's for Thanksgiving. There was lots of delicious food and plenty of talking, singing and teasing. After dinner the kids–big and little–played games.

That's the way it used to be, thought Molly as she fought back tears. Grandpa McPherson had died two months ago, and Molly really missed him. How could she be happy and thankful when her wonderful grandfather wouldn't be there?

I'll just have to get through the day, Molly thought as they went into Grandma's house and were greeted by a ton of relatives. Soon it was time for dinner and the Thanksgiving prayer. But Grandpa always said the prayer. Who would do it this year?

Molly was surprised when she saw Grandma stand up and motion for quiet. Softly, she prayed, "Dear God, thank You for all the blessings You give us. Thank You for all the people who are here today and for the one we all miss, Grandpa. Thank You for all the love and fun he gave us. We are happy that Grandpa is spending this Thanksgiving in heaven with You and that we will be there, too, some day. Amen."

A smile spread across Molly's face as she thought of Grandpa.

Your Turn

1. For what are you most thankful?

_____

_____

2. Why is it important to thank God for His blessings?

_____

_____

Prayer

Lord, help me to be thankful for all I have. Amen.

Basket of Blessings

All the blessings in your life are gifts from God. The best gift is on the basket handle. Unscramble all the words and write them on the lines below. Add two blessings of your own on the empty lines. Thank God for each of these gifts.

1. _____ 2. _____ 3. _____

4. _____ 5. _____ 6. _____

7. _____ 8. _____ 9. _____

10. _____ 11. _____ 12. _____

_____ _____

The solution is on page 233.

Thankful

I should thank others for their help.

Give thanks to the Lord, call on his name; make known
among the nations what he has done.

~ Isaiah 12:4

Gratitude Attitude

Katie Arenson went to sleep thinking about twirling her baton and marching ahead of the band in the county fair parade the next day. The next morning, she practically flew out of bed when the alarm rang.

"Hi, Katie. Just in time," said her dad when she came into the kitchen.

"In time for what?"

Mr. Arenson raised his eyebrows. "In time to help with the animals."

Katie frowned and mumbled, "I'll be out in a minute."

One minute stretched into 30 as Katie dawdled over breakfast and thought of how cool she would look in her twirler's uniform. Her daydreaming was interrupted by the bang of the back door as her sister, Susie, stomped into the kitchen. "Well, Princess, at least you're up!" Susie said sarcastically.

"What's her problem?" Katie asked their dad.

"Maybe Susie didn't like doing all the barn work alone this morning."

"Uh…guess I was thinking about the parade," Katie stammered.

"I'm sure you thanked your sister for doing your work," said Mr. Arenson.

"Uh…" Katie looked embarrassed. "Well, she shouldn't get so mad! I didn't ask her to do it. She volunteered."

"You think that if a person volunteers to do something she shouldn't be thanked?" questioned Mr. Arenson. "I think you need to improve your gratitude attitude. Anything someone does for you is worthy of thanks."

Your Turn

1. Have you ever forgotten to thank someone for what he or she did for you? How do you think that person felt to not be thanked?

_____

_____

2. Why is it important to say thank you to people and to God?

_____

_____

Prayer

Lord, help me to have an attitude of gratitude. Amen.

Thanks, God

God gives us many blessings every day. Fill in the journal page with words that tell how God has blessed you.

Dear Journal,
When I looked out my window this morning, I enjoyed seeing _____.
I got dressed and put on _____ and _____. I'm glad to live with _____. When I was hungry, I ate _____.
I worked on _____ and played with _____.
I also enjoyed these other blessings from God:

_____
_____
_____
_____
_____
_____
_____
_____
_____

Thankful

I should be content with what I have.

Be content with what you have.

~ Hebrews 13:5

Is That All?

What a mess! It looked like Tornado Christmas had touched down right in the family room. Paper, ribbons, bows and empty boxes littered the floor.

Marcy Wilkens' little brother, Joey, was having a great time running his new fire engine through paper tunnels and around box buildings. Marcy's mom was smiling and looking through a book she had received. Mr. Wilkens was laughing as he took a sneak peek at the video he had taken out of the package.

Marcy checked the far corners under the tree once more. Then she gave a big sigh as she realized it just wasn't there. "Is something bothering you?" asked her mom. "Don't you like your gifts?"

"Oh, Mom, these are really cool gifts, but…" Marcy stuttered.

"But you didn't get the CD boom box you wanted," Mom finished for Marcy. "I'm sorry you're disappointed, but the Bible reminds us that we should be content with what we have. And remember that in the birth of Jesus we have the greatest gifts of all time: love and forgiveness."

Marcy gave her mom a hug before she went to her room to listen to her new CDs on her old CD player.

Your Turn

1. What things make you feel discontented like Marcy?

_____

_____

2. Why is it important to be content with what you have?

_____

_____

Prayer

God, help me to be content with what I have and not keep wanting more. Amen.

The Greatest Gift

Think of the most awesome gift you ever received. How did you feel when you got it? Do you still have it? Do you still like it? God gave you a gift that is thousands of times more awesome than anything you have ever received. And it never gets too small or wears out. Want to find out what that gift is? Decode the message on this package, by crossing out these letters: G J K M P Q X Z. Write the remaining letters, in order, on the lines. The solution is on page 233.

_____

_____

Faithful

Faithfulness involves remembering responsibilities.

But when the Holy Spirit controls our lives, he will produce this kind of fruit in us: love, joy, peace, patience, kindness, goodness, faithfulness.

~ Galatians 5:22 NLT

Faithful or Forgetful?

"And just where do you think you're going, Joelle?"

Joelle Frederickson turned as she heard her stepmother's voice. Her hand was on the side doorknob. "I was going next door to Jill's to see her kittens," she replied.

"You haven't taken Spotty out for his walk, nor have you fed him this morning." Mrs. Carver pointed to the terrier laying on her mat near the stove.

Joelle sighed, which caused her light brown bangs to flutter. "Oh, Jane. Can't I do that when I get back?" She knew that request was hopeless when she saw the firm look on her stepmother's face.

"Joelle, you promised you'd take care of the dog if we got her for you."

"Okay, okay!" Joelle sighed as she moved to feed Spotty. "I'm sorry I forgot about you, girl."

Spotty licked the back of her hand as if to say, "I forgive you."

Joelle smiled. "Jane's right. You are faithful, even when I'm not."

Your Turn

1. Was Joelle faithful or forgetful? Explain.

_____

_____

2. Are you faithful or forgetful about tasks for which you are responsible? Explain why.

_____

_____

Prayer

Father God, I need Your help to be faithful. Amen.

The Reward for Faithfulness

Want to know the reward for faithfulness? The following puzzle is a verse from the Bible. To find the verse, put the letters below each column in the boxes above that column, then read across. The letters may not be listed in the exact order in which they appear in the quote. Mark off used letters at the bottom. A letter may only be used once. The black boxes stand for the end of a word.

The solution is on page 233.

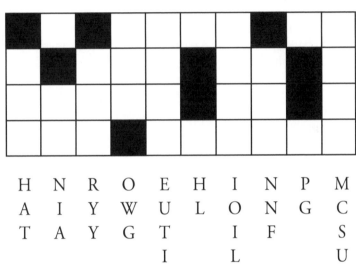

H	N	R	O	E	H	I	N	P	M
A	I	Y	W	U	L	O	N	G	C
T	A	Y	G	T		I	F		S
				I		L			U

Faithful

I will be faithful, even when others aren't.

If anyone is ashamed of me and my words...the Son of Man will be ashamed of him when he comes in his Father's glory with the holy angels.

~ Mark 8:38

A Faithful Friend?

"Ugh." Sherise Miller tossed the tract that she had just been handed into the garbage. "I'm sick of those."

Laura Silvers glanced at the tract. It was one that her Sunday school class had once given out. She glanced at Sherise, wondering if she should say something.

"Don't you just hate it when people give out those things?" Sherise asked. "My mother says that people shouldn't try to force you to believe in God. That's why we don't go to church."

Laura didn't say anything. Then she remembered the promise she had made in church that Sunday to be faithful to God even when others weren't. Now there she was with Sherise, one of the most popular girls in sixth grade. Laura felt like being friends with Sherise made her more popular.

"Want to sleep over Saturday night?" Sherise asked. "You can go out to breakfast with us on Sunday morning."

Laura hesitated to answer. Her family went to church on Sundays. She knew that her mother would say no to the sleepover. She didn't know what to tell Sherise about why her mother would say no.

Your Turn

1. If Laura doesn't say anything about God, whom is she showing more faithfulness to: Sherise or God? Why?

_____

_____

2. How do you show faithfulness to God? Why is faithfulness important?

_____

_____

Prayer

Lord Jesus, help me to be faithful to You, no matter what. Amen.

A Sign of Your Faithfulness

Many people use signs to show what their companies or causes are all about. Use the sign below to draw or use words to show how you're faithful to God.

Faithful

God offers His protection and power to help me be faithful.

He [God]…protects the way of his faithful ones.

~ Proverbs 2:8

The Way of the Faithful

Every Saturday at 9 a.m., Molly Halvorsen walked Mrs. Herman's dog. Mrs. Herman was her 86-year-old next-door neighbor. Molly and her best friend, Lisa, took turns walking the dog. Normally, Mrs. Herman could walk the dog herself. But after having surgery, she did not get out much.

One Saturday, Molly almost called to say that she wouldn't be able to walk Snapper, Mrs. Herman's frisky German shepherd. All night long the snow had fallen. With the cold wind blowing, the ground also had a covering of ice. But Molly knew that God would want her to be faithful.

"There are at least four inches of snow on the ground," Molly's older brother said as he headed out the door on his way to hockey practice.

Oh, great! Molly grumbled to herself. *I wish Mrs. Herman could have at least put salt down to melt the snow. I wish this was Lisa's day to walk Snapper.*

The wind rushed to meet her as she stepped outside. It was so cold, Molly felt like her braces were in deep-freeze mode! But as Molly left her house, she noticed that instead of slippery snow, the ground had been freshly shoveled. In fact, the snow had been shoveled all the way to the end of the block–her usual route with Snapper.

"I knew you'd come," Mrs. Herman said as Molly walked into the house to get Snapper. "I had the neighbor boys shovel out a path for you. They put salt down so you wouldn't slip."

Thanks, God, Molly thought.

Your Turn

1. How was Molly faithful?

_____

_____

2. How did God "protect [her] way"?

_____

_____

Prayer

Thank You, dear Lord, for protecting my way. Amen.

Jesus' Promise

Jesus promised to help you be faithful. John 14:26 tells you how. To figure out the message, read the grid coordinates. Fill in the letters on the blanks. (For example, 4,8 is Y.) The first number is always the bottom number. **Hint:** Some letters are in two places.

The solution is on page 233.

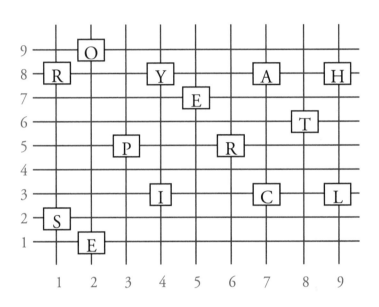

The ____ ____ ____ ____ ____ ____ , the
    9,8   2,1   9,3   3,5   5,7   6,5

____ ____ ____ ____ ____ ____ ____ ____ ____
9,8   2,9   9,3   4,8   1,2   3,5   4,3   1,8   4,3   8,6

will ____ ____ ____ ____ ____ you everything.
    8,6   2,1   7,8   7,3   9,8

Obedient

I should obey God and my parents out of love.

Then he [Jesus] went down to Nazareth with them and was obedient to them.

~ Luke 2:51

Listening and Doing

"Are you listening to me?"

Amber really didn't like it when her mother said that. "Yes, I'm listening," she said. She tried to shove a dirty sock under her bed as her mom stood in the doorway of her room.

"Excellent," Mom said. "I suggest you not only listen, but also act. I want this room completely cleaned up and the dirty clothes sloshing around in the washer by the time I get back from grocery shopping. Or else!"

Amber nodded as she surveyed the disaster area. She knew that tone. Her mom wasn't really suggesting that she get busy–she expected her to do it! She knew what "or else" meant: grounded for a week. No TV or phone privileges. Amber also knew this wasn't the first time her mom had told her to clean up.

As Amber started picking up her stuff, she noticed a devotional book her mother had given her. That day's entry was titled "Obeying God."

Obey, obey, obey, she thought. *Everyone wants me to obey.*

Then she noticed another word: love.

Amber knew her mother loved her, even though she expected her to do this job. *Maybe God is like that, too,* she thought as she gathered dirty clothes from the floor, chairs and closet.

Your Turn

1. How are you obeying God when you obey your parents?

_____

_____

2. What do you find hard and/or easy about obeying?

_____

_____

Prayer

Lord, help me to obey You and my parents. Amen.

Ways to Obey

Figure out which letter to place below each picture, and then rearrange those letters to name three ways to obey God. Example: the first picture is a desk. The number 1 indicates the first letter of the word "desk" which is "d."

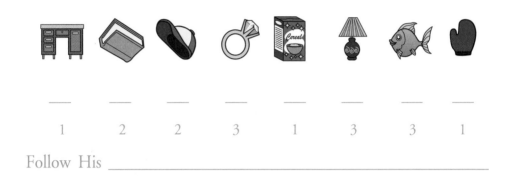

1	2	2	3	1	3	3	1

Follow His _____

—

4	2	3	4	5	1	2

Obey my _____

—

1	4	4	3	1	3	5	5

Tell others the _____ .

The solution is on page 233.

Obedient

I should put God first in my life.

We must obey God rather than men!

~ Acts 5:29

A True Score

Shawna and Kelsey lived on neighboring farms about 20 miles from Haskins Middle School. They usually spent the hour-long bus ride to school chatting, but this morning's ride was different. Kelsey could tell Shawna was upset as soon as she slid into the seat next to her.

"Are you sick?" Kelsey asked.

"Don't I wish! Then I could miss the science test today," Shawna said. Mr. Nelson, their science teacher, had made it clear that this was an important test.

"Yeah, I know," Kelsey sighed. "I've been studying for days. I feel like my brain is ready to burst."

Shawna looked like she could cry. "My brain is empty and hollow. Not one scientific fact in it! I kept putting off studying. I was going to cram it all in last night. But I forgot my book at school. Then I couldn't sleep. Now I'm tired and stupid!"

Kelsey thought for a minute, then said, "I know! I'll write really big. When you don't know an answer, look over at my paper and copy it. No one will know."

Kelsey's so smart, thought Shawna. *She'll probably know all the answers. It would be easy.*

Then Shawna shook her head. "I can't do that," she said. "It would be cheating, and cheating is the same as stealing. Stealing is wrong."

Kelsey just shrugged her shoulders. "Whatever!" she said.

Your Turn

1. Has your disobedience ever caused trouble for you or someone else? What happened?

_____

_____

2. Has your obedience ever prevented trouble? What did you do and what happened?

_____

_____

Prayer

Lord, help me to trust You enough to obey. Amen.

Why Obey?

Obedience is sometimes difficult. We like to feel that we are in charge of situations and can do things on our own. But there's a good reason why God wants us to obey Him. Use the grid to figure out why. The first number is always the one on the bottom.

The solution is on page 233.

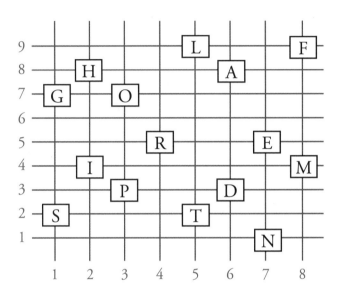

$\overline{}$ $\quad$ $\overline{}$ $\overline{}$ $\qquad$ $\overline{}$ $\overline{}$ $\overline{}$ $\qquad$ $\overline{}$ $\overline{}$ $\overline{}$ $\overline{}$ $\overline{}$
2,4 $\quad$ 6,8 8,4 $\qquad$ 5,2 2,8 7,5 $\qquad$ 8,9 2,4 4,5 1,2 5,2

$\overline{}$ $\overline{}$ $\overline{}$ $\quad$ $\overline{}$ $\qquad$ $\overline{}$ $\overline{}$ $\qquad$ $\overline{}$ $\overline{}$ $\overline{}$
6,8 7,1 6,3 $\quad$ 2,4 $\qquad$ 6,8 8,4 $\qquad$ 5,2 2,8 7,5

$\overline{}$ $\overline{}$ $\overline{}$ $\overline{}$; $\overline{}$ $\overline{}$ $\overline{}$ $\overline{}$ $\overline{}$ $\qquad$ $\overline{}$ $\overline{}$ $\overline{}$ $\overline{}$ $\quad$ $\overline{}$ $\overline{}$
5,9 6,8 1,2 5,2 $\quad$ 6,8 3,3 6,8 4,5 5,2 $\qquad$ 8,9 4,5 3,7 8,4 $\quad$ 8,4 7,5

$\overline{}$ $\overline{}$ $\overline{}$ $\overline{}$ $\overline{}$ $\overline{}$ $\overline{}$ $\overline{}$ $\overline{}$ $\overline{}$ $\overline{}$. Isaiah 44:6
5,2 2,8 7,5 4,5 7,5 $\quad$ 2,4 1,2 $\quad$ 7,1 3,7 $\quad$ 1,7 3,7 6,3

Obedient

God will help me tell others the Good News.

He [Jesus] said to them, "Go into all the world and preach the good news to all creation.

~ Mark 16:15

Too Scary!

"It's too scary. I just can't do it!" exclaimed Kendall.

"Are you talking about the new roller coaster at Fun World?" asked her mother. "I know you kids have been thinking about it all week."

"No, no. I was thinking about something entirely different than the roller coaster. I was thinking about how scared I would be to just walk up to a complete stranger and start preaching about Jesus."

Mrs. Baker looked surprised. "Why do you need to do that?"

Kendall answered, "My Sunday school teacher, Miss Markson, said thousands of people don't know about Jesus. Christians are supposed to obey God. Jesus said to preach the Good News to everyone in the entire world."

Her mother said, "Kendall, there are lots of ways to obey Jesus' command to spread the Good News about His love. You can invite someone to church or Sunday school. You can pray. You can give money for missions. And you can start with people you know."

"Whew!" Kendall said. "I think I'll ask Uncle Tom to go to church with us next week. And I could ask Aleesha to go to Sunday school with me."

Your Turn

1. Do you ever feel like Kendall when you think about what God wants you to do? What do you do about it?

_____

_____

2. Do you find it difficult to be obedient to God? Why or why not?

_____

_____

Prayer

Heavenly Father help me to obey Your command to spread the Good News of Jesus to others. Amen.

Following and Obeying

The Bible is full of people who followed and obeyed God. Sometimes their obedience caused them to have many problems or even be put to death. Find the names of some of these people in the word search below.

The solution is on page 234.

```
D  D  A  N  I  E  L  I  M  U  D

I  Y  J  O  B  C  E  S  R  M  G

V  B  E  S  N  A  U  A  E  A  I

A  B  R  A  H  A  M  I  T  R  D

D  O  E  C  O  S  A  A  E  Y  E

L  R  M  R  J  I  S  H  P  O  O

A  U  I  O  A  C  T  O  A  U  N

S  T  A  D  B  S  S  E  S  O  M

A  H  H  P  E  S  O  J  E  A  N
```

ABRAHAM	JOB
ASA	JOHN
DANIEL	JOSEPH
DAVID	MARY
DORCAS	MOSES
ESTHER	NOAH
GIDEON	PAUL
JEREMIAH	PETER
ISAAC	RUTH
ISAIAH	SAMUEL

Prayerful

God hears all my prayers.

Call upon me in the day of trouble; I will deliver you.

~ Psalm 50:15

What Can I Say?

Diana Jurgens was very quiet on the way home from Sunday school with her mom. She slumped in the seat and stared out the window.

Finally, Mrs. Jurgens said, "Diana, you seem really upset. Do you want to talk about it?"

Diana let out a big sigh as she told her mom what was bothering her. "It's the same old thing," she said. "Our lesson today was about worship and going to church. All I could think of was Dad and how he never goes to church. I love Dad and I want him to go to church with us. It's great when he goes on special occasions like Christmas or Easter, but I want him to go all the time."

"Maybe you should talk to your father about it," her mom said.

Diana shook her head. "I do talk to him. I ask him to come with us and he says he's busy or he's tired. Sometimes he says he'll think about it. What else can I say?" she asked.

"I mean your other father–your heavenly Father," said Mrs. Jurgens. "He always listens. Ask for His help in talking to Dad."

"Can we pray right now?" asked Diana. Her mom answered by pulling off to the side of the road and turning off the car.

Your Turn

1. What do you need to pray about?

_____

_____

2. What does God promise in the Scripture at the top of this page?

_____

_____

Prayer

Heavenly Father, thanks for listening to my prayers and helping me. Amen.

Prayer Pretzels

The first pretzels were made as a tasty treat for kids who learned their prayers. The pretzels were shaped to look like the crossed arms of someone praying. When you eat pretzels, think of how you can bring anything to Jesus in prayer.

Have an adult help you make some pretzels of your own from this recipe.

Prayer Pretzels
4 cups flour
4 tablespoons sugar
1 teaspoon salt
1 package yeast
1½ cups warm water
1 egg, beaten

1. Combine the yeast and water. Let stand for 5 to 10 minutes.

2. Add the egg, flour, salt and sugar.

3. Knead the dough on a lightly-floured surface until a smooth ball forms.

4. Ask an adult to preheat the oven to 425 degrees.

5. Roll the dough into 24 balls for small pretzels, 16 balls for larger pretzels.

6. Flatten each ball into thin strips about 10 inches long.

7. Shape the strips into pretzels by crossing the ends to make a loop, then flipping the ends back across the loop. Sprinkle with salt.

8. Place on lightly-greased baking sheets.

9. Ask an adult to bake the pretzels 15 to 20 minutes. Yummy!

Prayerful

Prayer holds my Christian life together.

The prayer of a righteous man is powerful and effective.

~ James 5:16

Spiritual Glue

Each student in the sixth-grade Bible study was given a word to explain at the next class. Karina's word was "prayer." *I already know how to pray,* she thought.

Karina was still thinking about it when Aunt Linda called. "Can you help me work on my crafts for the Easter Craft Fair?" her aunt asked.

Soon Karina and Aunt Linda were busy gluing arms, legs and other body parts on rabbits, chicks and ducks. They chatted while they put together the creatures.

"What's new with you, Karina?" Aunt Linda asked.

Karina said, "Not much. You know, same old thing: school, home and friends. Wait. There is something new in Bible study. But my part is pretty much the same old thing there, too." Karina explained her word assignment.

"I've been praying forever," said Karina. "What else is there to know?"

Aunt Linda told Karina to look at the finished wooden Easter figures that were carefully drying on the table. "What's the most important part of these animals?" she asked.

"Patterns and cutting them out exactly," Karina decided.

"That's important," her aunt agreed. "But the most important part of these crafts is the glue. Without the glue, nothing could be completed–they would just be a pile of pieces. Prayer is a sort of spiritual glue. It holds your Christian life together. Prayer is having a heart-to-heart talk with God. You can talk to Him about anything and everything."

Karina asked to borrow a rabbit to use in her explanation of prayer.

"Sure, hop to it," laughed Aunt Linda.

Your Turn

1. When do you pray?

_____

_____

2. Why is prayer important in a Christian's life?

_____

_____

Prayer

God, I'm glad I can always talk to You in prayer. Thanks for listening. Amen.

Prayerful Hands

Many times we fold our hands when we pray—it helps to keep them from doing other things and distracting us. Some people raise their hands when they pray. Here is another activity that connects your hand and prayer. Look at your hand and use your fingers to remind you of people in your life who need your prayers.

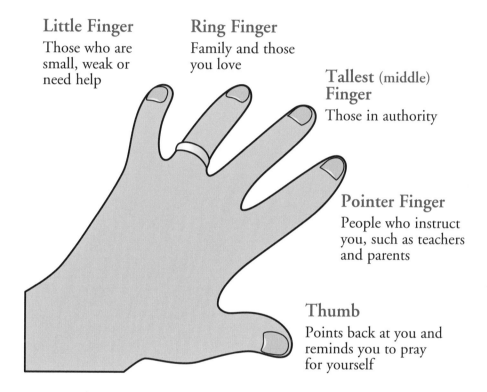

Little Finger
Those who are small, weak or need help

Ring Finger
Family and those you love

Tallest (middle) **Finger**
Those in authority

Pointer Finger
People who instruct you, such as teachers and parents

Thumb
Points back at you and reminds you to pray for yourself

Think of whom you are reminded by each finger and say a silent prayer for every one!

Prayerful

I can bring anything to God in prayer.

Do not be anxious about anything, but in everything, by prayer and petition, with thanksgiving, present your requests to God.

~ Philippians 4:6

Turn Off the News!

Brianna walked into the family room just as her dad turned on the evening news. "Could we please watch something else?" she asked. "Maybe there's something better on Channel 15."

But Mr. Hanson did not change the channel, so Brianna started to leave the room. "Wait a minute," said her dad. "You don't have to leave just because you can't see what you want."

Brianna quickly explained, "Oh, Dad. I'm not mad because you didn't change channels. It's just that watching the news makes me feel scared and sad. I hate seeing and hearing about murders, floods, wars and all the other terrible things. Maybe if I never watched TV it would be better."

"Well, I don't think you'll do that," Mr. Hanson answered. "Not seeing or hearing about bad news won't make it go away. As long as people are sinful, all kinds of terrible things will keep right on happening. But there is something we can do about it."

Brianna asked, "What's that?"

"We can pray for those people. God wants us to pray about everything. He promises to hear our prayers and help those in need," he said.

Brianna and her father bowed their heads and asked God for help.

Your Turn

1. How do you react to distressing news stories that you hear or read?

_____

_____

2. How can you help people you don't know?

_____

_____

Prayer

Loving God, please help and comfort people who are having trouble. Amen.

Praying For Others

God promises to hear our prayers and to help those who are in need. If you read about someone in the newspaper or hear about someone on TV who needs God's help, pray for him or her. You can pray for anyone, even people you don't know. God knows everyone in the whole world. He wants us to pray for each other and for anyone who has trouble. Fill in the blanks of the prayer below. Use it as you pray for others, or make up your own prayer.

Dear God,
Sometimes I feel sad or scared or angry when I hear or read about all the terrible things that happen in the world. Today I want to pray for:

_____

Because this has happened to that person:

_____

Please help my friend and be with him or her. Thank You, God, for Your love for all people. In Jesus' name. Amen.

Trusting

God wants me to trust Him.

Trust in the Lord with all your heart
Don't depend on your own understanding.

~ Proverbs 3:5 ICB

Trust Exercise

"Okay, let's try a trust exercise."

Everyone groaned when the youth pastor made that announcement.

"Now what?" Sharon Pete whispered to her friend Lacey Jameson. "Remember last week when he had us fall back into each other's arms?"

Lacey nodded. Nobody had wanted to do that at first. The feeling was confirmed when Jason Myers failed to catch Patricia Hawkes. Everyone had gasped when she crashed to the floor.

The youth pastor surprised them by announcing, "I want everyone to think of one thing that worries you the most."

Sharon instantly thought of her upcoming science quiz. She had to pass it or get an F for the year.

"Got something? Good. Now give it totally to God. Just stop worrying about it. Trusting God is the opposite of worrying."

Sharon exchanged a glance with Lacey. *That's easy to say*, she thought.

"That's easy to say, right?" the youth pastor said, as if he had read Sharon's mind. "But we worry because we're leaning on our own understanding about a problem. That's not what God wants us to do."

Sharon sighed.

Your Turn

1. What does it mean to "trust in the Lord with all your heart"?

_____

_____

2. What worries you? Use the prayer below to give it to the Lord.

_____

_____

Prayer

Lord, I'm worried about _____. Help me to trust You about it. Amen.

Trust Old Testament Style

Many people in the Old Testament showed their trust in God. Solve the crossword to find out some of them.

Across

The solution is on page 234.

1. She watched her little brother float down the Nile.
4. This man trusted God to give him a son in his old age. (Genesis 17:5, 21)
6. This man was afraid to lead 2 Down against the Midianites. (Judges 6)
8. He trusted God to help him rebuild the walls of Jerusalem. (Neh. 2:11-18)
10. Wife of 4 Across.

Down

2. This nation trusted God.

3. This man believed that God would help him defeat a giant. (1 Samuel 17)

5. This woman believed that God would give her a son. (1 Samuel 1)

7. This woman went into battle believing that God would help her. (Judges 4)

9. This queen fasted and prayed for the courage to face a king.

Trusting

God helps me choose whom to trust.

Trust in him at all times, O people.

~ Psalm 62:8

Too Trusting?

"I told you! I told you not to trust her."

If there was one thing Jenna Petersen hated, it was hearing "I told you so." Her older sister, Brianna, was good at saying that. Jenna was almost sorry she had told Brianna about Sarah. At 16, Brianna seemed like a know-it-all at times.

Still, she could hardly believe what Sarah had done. Sarah had stolen Jenna's idea for the school spirit poster contest. Jenna had shown Sarah the poster she planned to enter in the contest. But the next thing she knew, Sarah had copied the poster and entered the contest herself.

Jenna sighed. "I thought I could trust her. After all, she's my friend." She glanced at Brianna with tear-filled, green eyes.

Brianna snorted. "Some friend! You just hoped she'd be your friend because you think she's so cool and all. But what did she ever do to earn your trust?"

Jenna thought about that. She couldn't think of anything. She had only known Sarah since the new school year started three months ago.

"It doesn't pay to be too trusting! Well…in most cases. There's only one person you can always trust, no matter what."

Jenna thought she knew the answer, but decided to let her sister say it. "Who?"

"God."

Your Turn

1. How did Sarah betray Jenna's trust?

_____

_____

2. Has a friend ever done that to you? How did you feel?

_____

_____

Prayer

Jesus, I put my trust totally in You. Amen.

 # Trust New Testament Style

You solved a crossword puzzle on the Old Testament in the previous reading. Now let's move on to the New Testament. Many people in the New Testament showed their trust in God, too. Solve the crossword to find out some of them.

Across

The solution is on page 234.

4. Jesus helped this _____ woman to trust Him as the Messiah. (John 4)
7. When this woman trusted Jesus, she opened her home to 2 Down. (Acts 16:14-15)
9. This helper of Jesus trusted Him enough to try to walk on water. (Matthew 24:28-29)
10. This apostle trusted Jesus enough to help 2 Down. (Acts 9:27)

Down

1. This apostle trusted Jesus after meeting Him on the road to Damascus. (Acts 9:1-9)
2. He trusted God to care for him even though he was in prison. (Acts 16:16-40)
3. This woman believed that Jesus was the Messiah and could help her brother Lazarus. (John 11:25-27)
5. This brother of 7 Across became a follower of Jesus, then introduced his brother to Him. (John 1:40)
6. This helper of Jesus wrote a Gospel to show his trust in God.
8. This woman believed that God would give her a son even though she had no husband. (Luke 1:26-38)

Stewardship

God wants me to be wise about my resources.

*Well done, good and faithful servant; you were faithful over a few things,
I will make you a ruler over many things.*

~ Matthew 25:21, 23 NKJV

A Good Steward (Part 1)

"Look! Grandma gave me $20 for my birthday!" Cate Banks said as she burst into the family room. There was a big grin on her freckled face as she proudly displayed the $20 bill. "Now I have enough to get those new inline skates that I wanted."

Her father glanced up from the newspaper. "What's wrong with your old pair?" he asked, pulling off his reading glasses.

"Daaaad! Everybody has the new Rollmatic 2000s."

"They cost over $160! There's nothing wrong with your old skates. You haven't had them a year."

"Daaaad!"

"Cate, remember we talked about being a good steward?"

Cate looked at the floor. "Yeah, but I didn't know what that meant."

"It means taking care of what God gives you. That includes being careful about how you spend money. It also means using what we have to help others."

Cate pouted. "You said I could spend my birthday money on whatever I wanted."

"If you spend all of your money on skates, do you think you're being a good steward?"

Cate wanted to say yes. Instead, she said nothing.

"What do you think you could do instead of buying those expensive skates?"

Your Turn

1. Why did her father think she wouldn't be a good steward if she followed her plan?

_____

_____

2. Answer Cate's father's question. What do you think Cate could do?

_____

_____

Prayer

Teach me, Lord, to be a good steward over everything that I have. Amen.

58

What Would You Do?

Pretend you have the $20 that Cate has. What would you do with it? Use the space below to draw a picture or describe it in words.

Stewardship

God gives me the ability to wisely use the resources with which He blesses me.

God has given each of you some special abilities; be sure to use them to help each other, passing on to others God's many kinds of blessings.

~ 1 Peter 4:10 TLB

A Good Steward (Part 2)

"Where are you off to?"

Cate Banks turned as she heard her best friend Jake's voice. "I'm going to tutor Mrs. Frankel's nephew in math." She nodded toward where Mrs. Frankel lived two houses away. Mrs. Frankel's nephew, Mark, had recently come to live with her and attend Cate's school.

Jake's mouth dropped open as he gazed at her over his glasses. "Tutor? You? I thought you hated doing that."

Cate shrugged. She felt a little reluctant to tell her best friend that she was trying to be a good steward. She knew that he'd only say, "What???!"

"So, what's the deal, Cate? You like him or something?"

Cate blushed to the roots of her carrot-colored hair. "No! I'm just…trying to do something to help someone."

"You like him." Jake sounded confident of that.

"I do not!" Cate screamed. She shook her head. Jake wouldn't understand.

"So, why are you doing this?"

She didn't know where to begin. She knew that she had always been good at math. It just came easily to her. Her mother reminded her of that one day, and that's why she decided to tutor. "It's a long story. If you're home, maybe I'll tell you all about it when I come back."

Your Turn

1. How did Cate plan to be a good steward?

_____

_____

2. Why is being a good steward important?

_____

_____

Prayer

I want to do my part to help others, Lord. Please show me what to do. Amen.

What Can You Do?

How will you use your talents to help others? You can come up with a plan of action below.

My idea list:

What I can do:

What I will do to help others:

Loving Others

Accepting

Believing in Jesus means accepting His sacrifice for me.

Present your bodies a living sacrifice, holy, acceptable to God,
which is your reasonable service.

~ Romans 12:1 NKJV

I Don't Accept!

"I just can't accept that! You just don't wanna be my friend!" Faith yelled into the phone before slamming it down.

She soon realized that her Uncle Ned stood in the kitchen doorway staring at her. "It's Jenny," she explained, almost spitting the name out. Her brown eyes flashed angrily. "Her excuse this time for not wanting to come to my sleepover is that her family is having company."

"Why do you keep inviting her?" Uncle Ned asked.

Faith shrugged. She didn't want her uncle to know how much she wanted Jenny to be her friend.

"You know, you sounded just like your grandma did when you said you couldn't accept her excuse. Remember she had trouble accepting the fact that Jesus died for her sins? Some people are not as accepting as others."

"What does that mean?"

Uncle Ned walked into the kitchen. "Well, it takes longer for them to accept the truth about God. They make excuses like your friend Jenny did."

"Ex-friend…Why can't they just believe?"

"I wish I knew the answer to that."

Your Turn

1. What couldn't Faith's grandmother accept?

_____

_____

2. What do you have trouble accepting?

_____

_____

Prayer

Lord, help me to happily accept Your love and forgiveness. Let me be more willing to accept others the way You accept me. Amen.

I Do Accept

Mary was very accepting of God's plans for her. Use the code to find her message of acceptance. Would you respond this way?

The solution is on page 234.

~ Luke 1:38

Accepting

God helps me accept hardships that come my way.

*The Lord gave and the Lord has taken away; may
the name of the Lord be praised.*

~ Job 1:21

Karen's Cousin

Karen Webb paused outside her cousin's hospital room. She didn't know how to act toward her. What do you say to a 12-year-old who is dying of cancer?

As Karen walked into the room, Melissa sat up in bed and waved to her, smiling. Karen couldn't help feeling surprised at seeing the big smile on her cousin's thin, pale face.

I'd be miserable if I were her, Karen thought.

"I'm glad you came," Melissa said. "Where's your mom?"

"She stopped to talk to the nurse. So…how are you feeling?"

Melissa shrugged. "Okay. Hey, wanna watch some TV with me?"

Karen just looked at her. Didn't she know she was dying? How could she be so normal about it?

"Why are you so quiet?" Melissa asked. She shook her head. "Everybody's been that way ever since the doctor said I was gonna die."

Karen felt relieved that Melissa said the "D" word herself. She felt less awkward somehow.

"I think God is really mean to let this happen to you," Karen said. She couldn't understand why God would let her cousin die.

Melissa looked surprised. "I'm not mad at God anymore. I was at first. But now I know that this isn't God's fault." She shrugged.

Karen felt like crying.

Your Turn

1. Why was Karen's cousin able to accept this news?

_____

_____

2. Look at the Scripture at the top. Job accepted the hardships in his life. In one day, he lost just about everything. How would you have felt in his place?

_____

_____

Prayer

Lord, help me to accept Your will for my life. Amen.

A Way to Accept

Here is a message that can help you be accepting when hard times come. The solution is on page 234.

 – EP + S +  – B

H +  – C – T

Y +   –E + ST

INTERESTS –B

_____

_____

Accepting

Listening to godly advice is one way to accept God's grace.

Listen to advice and accept instruction, and in the end you will be wise.

~ Proverbs 19:20

The Gift

Madison Gordon burst into the house, her face glowing with excitement.

"Look what Mr. Wheeler just gave us, Dad," she said as she placed a handful of cash on the table where her father sat reading the newspaper.

"Sixty dollars?" her father said, his eyebrows raised.

"He said he wanted to help us since…well, since you lost your job last week."

Her father frowned, then snapped the paper to another page. "Take the money back. We're not doing that bad."

"But, Dad…"

"We just can't accept charity. We don't need it. We'll be fine." He handed the money to Madison.

Madison didn't understand why they couldn't accept the money. Then she had an idea.

"Hey, Dad, remember when you told me that God died for us and that His death was a free gift? We couldn't earn it. All we had to do was take it, right?"

Her father nodded.

Madison held out the money. "Why can't we just look at this like that?"

Her father sighed. "Okay, I get the message."

Your Turn

1. What was Madison's advice?

_____

_____

2. How has someone's advice helped you to accept the truth about something?

_____

_____

Prayer

God, help me to accept Your will for my life. Amen.

A Gift for You to Accept

Here is a gift God wants you to accept. Hold this paper so that it is level with your nose. Then turn the paper clockwise.

Friendly

Friends stick by each other.

There is a friend who sticks closer than a brother.

~ Proverbs 18:24

Forever Friends

Bang! went the door.

Crash! went the books.

Stomp, stomp! went footsteps up the stairs.

"I think Lola is home," Mrs. Turner said to Matt.

"Sounds more like a charging rhino," Matt commented. "Must have been a rough day in sixth grade. Think I'll make myself scarce until she cools off."

As Matt went out the back door, Lola marched into the kitchen muttering loudly, "And I thought she was my friend. Yeah, what a friend she is!"

"Sounds like someone made you angry," her mom said.

"I am so-o-o mad!" Lola fumed. "Good old Merri, my forever friend, is about to become an ex-friend."

Mrs. Turner looked surprised. "You and Merri have been friends since kindergarten," she said. "What on earth happened?"

Lola explained, "There's this new girl, Lisa, in sixth grade and it's like Merri has adopted her. Merri invites Lisa to eat lunch with us, be in our study group and then sit with us on the bus."

"It's fun to have a special friend, and I'm sure when you calm down, you'll see that hasn't changed," said Mom as she gave Lola a hug. "Merri was being friendly to Lisa to make her feel welcome in a new school. That doesn't mean Merri has dumped you as a friend. Maybe in time, all three of you will be friends."

Lola smiled. "Lisa seems nice. Maybe this can work."

Your Turn

1. What makes someone a good friend?

_____

_____

2. How are you friendly to others–even those you don't know very well?

_____

_____

Prayer

Jesus, thank You for being my friend. Help me to be friendly to others. Amen.

Jesus' Friends

Jesus is a friend to all people–no matter who they are. The Bible tells us about some of Jesus' friends. Their descriptions are printed below using code. To decode the words, remove the "ay" at the end of each word and then move the last remaining letter to the beginning of the word. For example, "undaysay choolsay" is "Sunday school."

The solution is on page 235.

Jesus was a friend of…

INNERSSAY _____

AXTAY OLLECTORSCAY _____

LINDBAY _____

AMELAY _____

OORPAY _____

EPERSLAY _____

HILDRENCAY _____

EGGARSBAY _____

Jesus is also a friend of _____ _____

(Write your name in code and then decode it.)

71

Friendly

Friends help each other.

If one falls down, his friend can help him up. But pity the man who falls and has no one to help him up!

~ Ecclesiastes 4:10

The Perfect Day

"Yahoo!" whooped Toneika as she hung up the phone. Her brother, Todd, almost got trampled underfoot as she danced around the kitchen.

"Have you gone completely ballistic?" he asked.

Out of breath, Toneika flopped into a chair. "Uncle Stu said I could invite six friends for a day at his ranch. He will take us trail riding and we can have a campfire dinner. It will be a perfect day–just horses and friends," she said.

"Hmm. Hard to tell who's more important to you, the horses or the friends."

Toneika ignored her brother. She absolutely loved everything about horses and horseback riding. She had been riding since she was four years old. Most of her friends were good riders, too.

"Who you gonna invite?" Todd asked.

Toneika hesitated. "Well, Sara, Tiffany, Michelle, and Paige would be fun."

"How about Liz? You can invite one more."

Toneika frowned. She knew she should invite Liz, but Liz was a terrible rider. She didn't ride much, so she was slow, cautious and always asking for help.

"I don't think so," Toneika finally mumbled.

Todd shook his head. "I guess horses are more important. With a friend like you, who needs enemies?" said Todd as he quickly left the kitchen while Toneika glared at him.

What does he know? thought Toneika. Then she remembered all the times Liz helped her at things she couldn't do very well.

Your Turn

1. If you were Toneika, would you invite Liz? Why or why not?

_____

_____

2. Why is it important to be a friend in all situations?

_____

_____

Prayer

Lord, I want to always stick with my friends. I can with Your help. Amen.

A Friendly Circle

It's great to have friends. Who are your friends? Cut a "circle of friends" to help you remember to thank God for His gift of friends.

What You Need

two contrasting colors of construction paper
scissors
pencil
glue
fine-tipped markers

What to Do

1. Cut two circles from two different colors of construction paper.
2. Fold one circle twice to make quarter circles.
3. Using the pattern below, trace half of a person on each fold.
4. Connect their arms.
5. Draw half a heart inside each person's body.
6. Cut out the shapes and hearts. Do not cut along the folds.
7. Unfold the circle and glue it to the other circle.
8. Glue the cutout hearts between the figures.
9. Write, "Friends are great!" around the circle. You may also write your friends' names on the hearts.

Friendly

Friends like each other even in bad times.

Never abandon a friend—either yours or your father's.

~ Proverbs 27:10 NLT

True Friends

Caitlyn felt her cheeks grow hot–she knew they were as red as a stoplight. *How could I be so stupid?* she thought. *I wish I could just disappear into thin air.* Instead, she had to walk across the auditorium stage and sit down.

Caitlyn had been the school spelling champ for two years. But today she had misspelled "handkerchief" and she was out of the spelling bee.

At lunch, Caitlyn sat in the far corner by herself. She kept her head down as she nibbled at her sandwich. Then Abigail scooted in next to her.

"Why are you sitting way over here?" she asked. "Come eat with the rest of us."

Caitlyn kept her head down as she mumbled, "I'm too embarrassed. I studied for weeks and then I bombed out on an easy word. The kids probably think I'm really stupid."

Abigail looked surprised. "Don't be S-I-L-L-Y, we know you can outspell us any day. Besides we're your F-R-I-E-N-D-S. And that's what friends are for. They like you all the time, even when you are upset or E-M-B-A-uh, embarrassed."

Caitlyn had to laugh as she gathered up her lunch and joined her friends. "Thanks, guys," she said. "You are true friends."

Your Turn

1. Why is it important to "never abandon" a friend?

_____

_____

2. How can you be a friend who never abandons another?

_____

_____

Prayer

Lord, I want to stick with my friends. I can with Your help. Amen.

Friendship Chain

Look closely at the design. All the names hook together. Maybe your name or the name of a friend is there. In the middle of the design is the name of your very best friend: Jesus. We can be friendly to others because Jesus is always a friend to us.

```
                                L
          S O N I A         B R I G I T
    I D A   U                   N     R
      O   E S T H E R     T   D   K A R I
      R     A           J O R D A N   C
    K I M   N A N       A   I     A   Y   A
    A     R   N     J E S U S       T       S
    T A R A   D   E   M   H     H A N N A H
    H     C H R I S T I N A       L         L
    R U T H   E   S   N           I         E
    Y       E   A   I   E         E M I L Y
    N       L       C
                    A
```

Make a name design of your own below, with Jesus' name in the center. Use the names of your family and friends. Be sure to include your own name!

Helpful

God wants me to help others.

Share with God's people who are in need. Practice hospitality.

~ Acts 12:13

A Dirty Job

"Whewy! What stinks?" gasped Erika.

"Smells like something died!" said her sister, Julia, as she held her nose.

They had just gotten off the school bus. The closer they got to the house, the worse the smell became. When they rounded the corner to the back yard, they found the "stinker." A huge pile of mulch and compost had been dumped on a corner of the garden. Their mother was trundling a wheelbarrow full of the stuff to a corner flowerbed.

"Hi, girls," she said. "Isn't it a beautiful spring day?"

"Maybe if you put a clothespin on your nose," said Julia.

Their mother just laughed. Then she looked at the pile and said, "Three cubic yards of compost is a lot! It's going to take me forever to get all of this on my garden and flower beds."

While the twins were having a snack, they started talking about Mother's Day, which was on Sunday. After discussing several ideas for a gift, they settled on something special.

"Mom," said Erika. "We are going to give ourselves to you for Mother's Day. We'll borrow two wheelbarrows and help you move this smelly pile."

"It's a dirty job but somebody's got to do it," chimed in Julia. "Think you could find a few gas masks?"

Your Turn

1. How do you think the girls' mother felt about their helpfulness?

_____

_____

2. Think of someone who may need your help. How can you be helpful to him or her?

_____

_____

Prayer

Lord, show me how to be helpful to those around me, and then do it. Amen.

Bible Time Mothers

Match these Bible-time moms and kids by putting the correct "kid" letter by the mother. If you get stuck, use the Bible references for help.

1. Eve _____
   (Genesis 4:1)

2. Hagar _____
   (Genesis 16:15)

3. Sarah _____
   (Genesis 21:3)

4. Rebekah _____
   (Genesis 25:21, 25-26)

5. Rachel _____
   (Genesis 35:24)

6. Jochebed _____
   (Exodus 6:20)

7. Ruth _____
   (Ruth 4:13-17)

8. Hannah _____
   (1 Samuel 1:20)

9. Bathsheba
   _____
   (2 Samuel 12:24)

10. Elizabeth _____
    (Luke 1:57-63)

11. Mary _____
    (Luke 2:5, 7, 21)

12. Eunice _____
    (2 Timothy 1:2, 5)

a. Samuel

b. Timothy

c. John

d. Solomon

e. Isaac

f. Joseph

g. Jacob, Esau

h. Ishmael

i. Cain

j. Moses

k. Obed

l. Jesus

The solution is on page 235.

Helpful

Encouraging words help others.

Do not let any unwholesome talk come out of your mouths, but only what is helpful for building others up according to their needs.

~ Ephesians 4:29

Way To Go!

Maren had watched her three older brothers play baseball from the time she was a toddler. As soon as she was old enough, Maren began playing on Little League teams herself.

She loved everything about baseball! Her first baseman's trapper mitt was her prized possession. She dreamed that someday she could play professional baseball in the major leagues.

Maren played for the Springfield White Sox. The team wasn't bad, but they weren't real good either. But that didn't matter to Maren. She always tried to do her best when she was playing first base and when she was batting.

Maren was also the team's cheerleader. She encouraged the pitcher from first base: "Way to go, girl. Two down and one to go. You can do it."

When she was sitting in the dugout, Maren talked up each batter. "Slow and steady. Keep your eye on the ball. Hit that baby."

One day after a game, Coach Wilson said to Maren, "I think your mouth gets as much of a workout as the rest of your body."

Oh, brother, thought Maren. *I've been talking too much. Guess I'd better tone it down.*

Then the coach surprised her by saying, "Your words make your teammates feel good about themselves. You're an encouragement. Keep it up!"

Your Turn

1. How do you feel when someone says kind or encouraging words to you?

_____

_____

2. Who can you encourage by what you say or do?

_____

_____

Prayer

Lord Jesus, help me to say helpful, kind and encouraging words to those around me. Amen.

Dori and Emily

Here is Dori the Discourager and Emily the Encourager. Dori always looks for faults and failings in people. Emily looks on the positive side and tries to be helpful in what she says. What do you think Emily would say in each of these situations?

Dori: I've told you 10 times how to do these math problems. Why can't you learn it?

Emily: _____

_____

_____

Dori: What is that supposed to be a painting of? I can't recognize anything on it.

Emily: _____

_____

_____

Dori: I think you need batting practice. You left two girls on base when you struck out.

Emily: _____

_____

_____

Dori: Your clothes are okay, I guess. Where did you say you got them?

Emily: _____

_____

_____

Helpful

Helping others can be a happy experience.

We must help the weak, remembering the words the Lord Jesus himself said:
"It is more blessed to give than to receive."

~ Acts 20:35

A Pleasant Surprise

"Exciting news!" Mr. Simons announced to the fifth-grade Sunday school class. "We are to have the honor of visiting Manor View nursing home every other Sunday for the next two months. It will be fun singing for the residents and visiting with them!"

Exciting, honor, fun? thought Aubrey. *Those aren't exactly the words I'd use to describe being with a lot of sick, old people.*

On the first visit, Aubrey watched the residents during the songs. Some were sleeping, some tapped their feet or clapped and some just smiled.

After they had finished singing, Mr. Simons paired off the kids and the residents. He introduced Aubrey to a white-haired lady in a wheelchair.

"Aubrey, meet Miss Hannah," he said. "Miss Hannah, Aubrey."

Miss Hannah was shrunken and twisted, but she had a wonderful smile. She reached out a gnarly hand to Aubrey and said in a tiny voice, "I'm so glad you came. I was a teacher for many years and I really miss working with the boys and girls. Now tell me all about yourself, your friends and school."

Aubrey soon forgot where she was. She was having a great time visiting with Miss Hannah and listening to her stories. Aubrey was surprised at how happy Miss Hannah was even though she couldn't do much.

When it was time to leave, Aubrey said, "I can't wait to come back next time. I'll bring pictures of my family and dog."

"I'll have some pictures, too," said Miss Hannah. "What fun we'll have!"

Your Turn

1. How was Aubrey helpful to Miss Hannah?

_____

_____

2. How was Miss Hannah helpful to Aubrey?

_____

_____

Prayer

Dear God, help me to notice those that need help and then help them. Amen.

God's Helper

You can be God's helper by helping those who are sad, lonely or in other bad situations. Look at each of these pictures and think of what you could do to help and what you could say to remind the people that God loves them and is with them.

_____

_____

_____

_____

_____

_____

_____

_____

_____

_____

_____

_____

Sincerity

I should be sincere in my actions and words.

We speak before God with sincerity, like men sent from God.

~ 2 Corinthians 2:17

A Big Phony?

"You're looking lovely today, Mom."

Brooke almost gagged when she heard her twin brother, Brett, compliment their mother in the hallway.

"Why thank you, Brett." Mrs. Gleason squeezed his shoulder as she went by.

"You phony!" Brooke hissed as Brett grinned. She felt tempted to grab a handful of his hair. "I know why you're being all nice to Mom. You're trying to butter her up so she'll let you go to the movies on Friday. But you're on punishment!"

Brett just continued to grin. Brooke rolled her eyes, then went in search of their mother. She was tempted to tell her mother what a phony Brett was. But she did not want to snitch, even though Brett deserved it.

Later that day, Brooke was about to enter the family room when she overheard her mother talking to Brett. "Brett, your father and I told you that you can't go to the movies. You're on punishment."

"Aw, Mom…"

"Honey, I've lived on this earth a lot longer than you have. Don't you think I know when you're being sincere and when you're up to something? You never compliment me unless you want something. Next time, try a little sincerity. You might get what you want."

Your Turn

1. Was Brett sincere or insincere?

_____

_____

2. Having sincerity means being honest in your actions. It doesn't mean flattering someone or pretending to be something you're not. Circle the answer below that describes you. Would someone say that you're sincere or insincere…

None of the time?   Some of the time?   Most of the time?   Why?

_____

_____

Prayer

Lord Jesus, help me to be sincere in my thoughts, words and actions. Amen.

A Lesson in Sincerity (Honest!)

Want to learn how to be sincere? Go through the word maze below. You'll find a message from Ephesians 5:1-2 (from the NIV Bible). Start at the first letter and keep going until you have connected every letter. Need a hint? The first word is TRY.

The solution is on page 235.

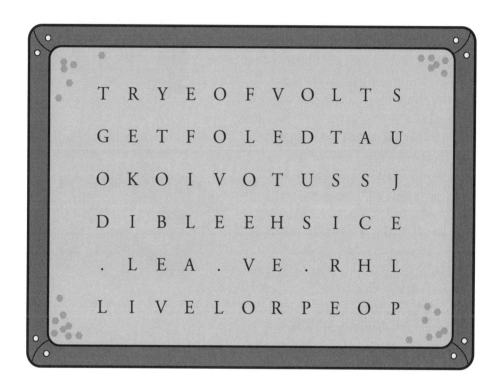

```
T  R  Y  E  O  F  V  O  L  T  S
G  E  T  F  O  L  E  D  T  A  U
O  K  O  I  V  O  T  U  S  S  J
D  I  B  L  E  E  H  S  I  C  E
.  L  E  A  .  V  E  .  R  H  L
L  I  V  E  L  O  R  P  E  O  P
```

83

Sincerity

God wants me to love others with sincere love.

Love must be sincere.

~ Romans 12:9

A Sincere Way to Love

Caroline came home in a snit.
If she saw Shannon once more, she'd have a fit.

Shannon was a girl she could not stand.
She played the piccolo in the school band.

Shannon made her life a tale of woe.
From morning 'til recess she bugged her so.

Shannon was in her sixth-grade class.
She once tripped Caroline as she tried to pass.

On Sunday, Caroline heard some bad news.
It threatened to change all of her views.

"You must love your enemies," her teacher said.
Those words filled Caroline with dread.

When the teacher said, "Love must be sincere,"
Caroline thought, *Okay, stop right here.*

I cannot love Shannon. She makes me sick.
To her I only can say sincerely, "Ick."

"I'll show you the way to truly love,"
her teacher said. "This love comes from God above.

"He is the key to hope so dear.
He'll love through you–never fear."

Now Caroline's heart felt truly glad.
God does all the work. That ain't so bad!

Your Turn

How would you feel if you were Caroline? Why?

_____

_____

Prayer

Lord, I want to have the sincere love that You have for others. Amen.

The Pledge

Cross out the Xs, Qs, Js and Zs to find a pledge you can take to be sincere. This pledge is a verse: Romans 12:10.

The solution is on page 235.

QBJEZ   JDEXQVJOTZEQD   TZOJ

_____   _____   ____

XOZNEQ   ZANJOXTQHEJR   JIQXN

_____   _____   ____

BQXROJTXHZEJRLXY   JLOQVXE.

_____   _____

ZHOXNOQRJ   JOZNQE

_____   _____

AXNOJTQHZERJ

_____

XAZBOQVJE   ZYOJURQSEJLXVEZSQ.

_____   _____

Sincerity

Praying with sincerity means wanting what God wants.

Let us draw near to God with a sincere heart in full assurance of faith.

~ Hebrews 10:22

Chelsea's Prayer

"God, if You can hear me, please help me to get an A on my next algebra quiz. I really need it. If You make sure I get an A, I promise I won't tease my sister for at least a week. Amen."

Just as Chelsea Liu ended her prayer, she thought of something else to add, "Your will be done. Amen."

She felt satisfied about her prayer until the day that she received her grade.

"C-!" she complained to her aunt when she arrived home.

Aunt June laughed. "At least you passed."

Chelsea ran a hand through her hair in frustration. Aunt June didn't understand anything! "I needed an A. That's what I prayed for! Now I'll get a D for the year."

"You said you prayed about this? What did you pray?"

Chelsea grabbed a bag of fruit snacks. "That I'd get an A. I even said, 'Your will be done,' like the Lord's Prayer says."

"And you think that's supposed to get you what you want from God?" Her aunt shook her head. "Did you study for the quiz? "

"Well...a little."

"That's not a very sincere prayer. For one thing, you just told God what you thought He wanted to hear. But those words aren't a magic formula. If you say, 'Your will be done,' that means you're willing to accept His answer, no matter what it is. Anyway, if you weren't willing to do your best as far as studying is concerned, then you can't blame God for the grade you received."

Your Turn

1. Do you think Chelsea meant what she prayed about her sister? Why or why not?

_____

_____

2. Have you ever prayed a prayer like Chelsea's? What was the result?

_____

_____

Prayer

Lord God, may I be sincere in all that I say or pray. Amen.

A Sincere Need

To be sincere, you'll need this. Color the shapes with the letters from the word SINCERE (turn the book so you can see it correctly).

You'll need a sincere _____.

The solution is on page 235.

Generous

God wants me to be generous toward others.

Remember this: The person who plants a little will have a small harvest.
But the person who plants a lot will have a big harvest.

~ 2 Corinthians 9:6 ICB

Share-o-Lot?

"Cassie, can I have some?"

Cassandra LaSalle groaned when she heard her little sister Kayla's voice. *Every time I get a candy bar she wants some,* she thought. She happened to have her favorite candy bar in the world: Chock-o-Lot. She didn't want to share it with her sister!

"I want to eat this myself," Cassandra decided.

Kayla skipped over to Cassandra's friend, the beads of her braids softly clicking. "Stephanie, can I have some of yours then?"

"Sure. Here you go." Stephanie broke off half of her candy bar.

Kayla skipped off to play with her friend Samantha. She returned to the porch ten minutes later with her hands behind her back. "I've got something for you," she said. "Guess which hand first."

Cassandra sighed loudly. "It's probably something stupid. Girl, go bother someone else."

"I wasn't talking to you." Kayla stuck out her tongue.

Stephanie tapped Kayla's left arm. Kayla nodded, then brought her hands forward. She held a cupcake in her hand covered with M&Ms.

"Samantha's mom just made these. She said I could give one away." Kayla skipped off once more.

As Cassandra sighed in annoyance, Stephanie turned aside to hide a grin.

Your Turn

1. What did Stephanie receive in return?

_____

_____

2. When it comes to sharing something you enjoy, are you like Cassandra or Stephanie? Why?

_____

_____

Prayer

Lord, sometimes I don't want to share what I have. Please give me the strength, courage and desire to share with others. Amen.

The Key to Generosity

Fill in the blanks to find what you need to be generous. The answer will appear in the outlined boxes. The solution is on page 235.

1. The size of the harvest you'll receive for planting a little. (See 2 Corinthians 9:6 on page 88.)

2. Amount of money that four quarters equal.

3. It is more blessed to _____ than to receive. (Acts 20:35)

4. This Son gave his life for you.

Generous

God gives back when I give.

Give, and you will receive. You will be given much. It will be poured into your hands—more than you can hold.

~ Luke 6:38 ICB

A Generous Return

Randi Patterson glanced at the two quarters in her hand. They were all she had to give in Sunday school. They were all the money she had, period.

It's not much, but at least I have something to give, she thought as she tossed them into the offering basket at the door. *Now I don't have any extra money to use at Temira's party. Oh, well.*

Temira's birthday party was held right after church at a pizza parlor. Invited kids lined up at a booth to buy tokens to play the arcade games. Randi hung around the table, talking to Temira's parents.

"Need some money for tokens?" Temira's father suddenly asked. He handed Randi $2 without waiting for an answer.

Randi thanked him, then ran off to play skee ball first. She was more than surprised when, after sinking her second ball, a blue light began to flash. Dozens of prize tickets came out of a small box at the end of the skee ball lane! Randi jumped up and down with excitement.

Your Turn

1. What did Randi give? What was she given in return?

_____

_____

2. Although you may give money in church, you may not always receive money in return. What else has God given you?

_____

_____

3. In what way will you be generous this week?

_____

_____

Prayer

Lord, help me to give; not just to receive, but to give from my heart. Amen.

What Will You Give?

Put a check in the box beside the item (time, talents, or money) that shows what you will give. Use the lines below to describe how you will use this item.

_____

_____

_____

_____

_____

_____

Generous

I should be generous without expecting anything in return.

Do good…be rich in good deeds, and…be generous and willing to share.

~ 1 Timothy 6:18

Smart and Generous?

Carrie Richards sighed. Sometimes, being so smart was such a curse. Yet tutoring others in math was expected of her as the best student in her fifth-grade class.

"Mom, you said you'd take me to Nick's so I can help him with his math homework," Carrie reminded her mother one Tuesday afternoon.

Her older sister, Shaelyn, glanced up from her sixth-grade math book. "Since when did you volunteer to help anyone?" she asked.

Carrie gave her a patient look as she brushed her blond hair out of her eyes. "I can't help it if I'm helpful."

Shaelyn laughed. "Yeah, right! You're up to something."

"I'm giving my time to help someone. Isn't that what the youth pastor said last Sunday?"

"I think you're being so generous because you heard that Nick has a copy of the new video game that you wanted to play."

Carrie left the room, not wanting to respond. But she knew that her sister was right.

Your Turn

1. Are you ever like Carrie? Why or why not?

_____

_____

2. A person who is willing to share doesn't look for what she can get from others. Think of ways you can share with others without looking for something in return. What will you share?

_____

_____

Prayer

God, You give me everything I have. Help me to be genuine as I share with others. Amen.

Rich in...What?

Besides good deeds, what do you think God wants you to be rich in (full of)? (No, we're not talking about money here!) To answer that question, first answer the questions below. Write your answers in the boxes. Then put the letters in the correct numbered boxes. The solution is on page 235.

1. This missionary who later traveled with the man at #4 generously gave money to the apostles. (Acts 4:36)

2. This woman and her husband pretended to be generous. (Acts 5:1-2)

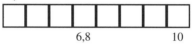

3. The prophet Elijah wanted this person from Zarephath to be generous. (1 Kings 17:9)

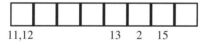

4. This apostle generously gave his time to spread the Gospel around the world. (Acts 13:13)

5. On page 90, you were told that if you do this, you will receive.

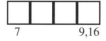

The  to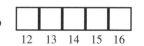

with others.

93

Honest

It is always best to be honest.

A good man is guided by his honesty; the evil man is destroyed by his dishonesty.

~ Proverbs 11:3 TLB

The Mistake

One Saturday, Kari, Jasmine and Brigit met at the mall for an afternoon of shopping. They were going to shop 'til they dropped…or until their mothers came to pick them up.

After having a snack, the three friends headed toward their favorite stores. They did a lot of looking and discussing before parting with their money. Kari found two CDs she really wanted, and Jasmine bought a fuzzy red sweatshirt.

"Brigit, what are you going to buy? You haven't spent a cent," said Kari.

"Let's go to Teen Town," she suggested. "I need some new jeans and maybe a sweater. They have some really fun clothes."

After much looking and trying on, Brigit found the perfect jeans. She also found a sweater she liked, but she didn't have quite enough money for both.

The girls decided to end their shopping trip with ice cream sundaes. As Brigit opened her wallet she said, "Something's wrong. I have too much money."

"What are you talking about?" asked Jasmine.

Brigit spread her money out on the table. "I should only have six dollars left, but I have eleven dollars. The cashier at Teen Town gave me five dollars too much. I need to take it back. Wait here for me."

"Are you crazy!" asked Kari. "Why take it back? It was her mistake. Now you can buy that sweater you like."

Brigit shook her head as she got up. "That wouldn't be honest," she said.

Your Turn

1. Why is it so important to be honest?

_____

_____

2. Is being honest easy or hard for you? Why?

_____

_____

Prayer

Lord, help me to be honest in everything I do and say. Amen.

Totally Honest

Jesus told a parable of a shrewd manager to teach a lesson about honesty. You can find it in Luke 16:1-12. Use this code to find out exactly how Jesus feels about cheating and being honest. The solution is on page 235.

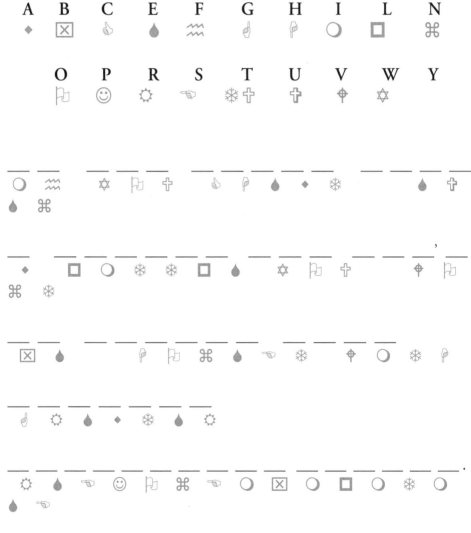

~ Luke 16:10 TLB

Honest

It is dishonest to lie.

You deserve honesty from the heart; yes, utter sincerity and truthfulness.

~ Psalm 51:6 TLB

The Music Story

Ellery did some quick thinking as she rushed around the corner and saw her mother's car in the driveway. What could she say to convince her that she had a good reason for being late? Ellery knew her mother would be upset if she knew Ellery had stopped at Lin's house and listened to CDs instead of coming straight home.

I'll say I had some music things to do after school, she decided. That was sort of true since she took five minutes to help Miss Bentley straighten the music room.

Ellery tried to slither into the house, but her mother called out, "Why were you so late?"

Ellery busied herself putting away her school things as she rattled off her explanation in one breath. After she had finished and was about to leave, her mother said, "Ellery, I've known you since you were born."

Ellery had to agree with that.

"Now why don't you start over and tell me the whole truth this time."

Ellery twisted her hair and blew out a big breath. "Well…" Then she blurted out the whole reason for her lateness.

Mother gave Ellery a long serious look. "Ellery, you know lying is wrong. When you only tell part of the story and not the whole truth, that's the same as lying. I don't like it when you keep things from me. Next time be completely honest."

Your Turn

1. When are you tempted to keep back part of the truth?

_____

_____

2. Why is not telling the whole truth the same as lying?

_____

_____

Prayer

Lord, help me to always tell the whole truth and nothing but the truth. Amen.

Lying Lips

God has something to say about lying and truthfulness in Proverbs 12:22. To discover the message, travel around this square. Starting at the arrow, write every other letter on the appropriate line. Go around two times. Answer is on page 235.

➡ T D H e e L L I O G R H D T

Left column (top to bottom): e L H U T f U H B T S U P

Right column (top to bottom): D S e I T N e M S e T N S I

Bottom row: R I T L e G R N A I O V H L

___ ____ _____

_____ ____ ___, ___ __ __

_____ __ ___ ___

___ _____ __ __. ~ Proverbs 12:22

Honest

I can be honest without using hurtful words.

A gentle answer turns away wrath, but a harsh word stirs up anger.

~ Proverbs 15:1

A Gentle Answer

"Look at me," said 5-year-old Moira as she twirled into Vanessa's bedroom.

"Why do you have those clothes on?" Vanessa asked as she surveyed her little sister's outfit. Moira was wearing a pink shirt with purple flowers with a blue and yellow plaid skirt. Red tights covered her legs, which ended in white sandals. Shiny beads were added for the finishing touch.

Moira was admiring herself in the mirror. "Aunt Sue and Uncle Ron are coming for dinner. I like them and I wanted to look pretty. What do you think?"

Words like "yuk," "terrible" and "go change your clothes" came to Vanessa's mind. She felt like any of them fit the vision before her. Vanessa was thinking of how pesty Moira could be and how she laughed at Vanessa's hair when she tried new styles. But the happy look on Moira's face stopped her words. She knew her sister was very proud of how she looked.

"You sure picked out a colorful outfit," she said, knowing that was an honest answer. "Aunt Sue and Uncle Ron will love it." That was honest, too, because their aunt and uncle loved them and always enjoyed visiting with them. They thought Moira was funny, and they would appreciate her bizarre outfit.

"Oh, goody! I can't wait to see them. Thanks, Nessa." Moira whooshed out of the room singing her favorite song.

Your Turn

1. Why do you think Vanessa didn't tell Moira exactly what she thought?

_____

_____

2. How can you give an honest, yet gentle, answer?

_____

_____

Prayer

Father, I want to be honest, but I don't want to hurt people. Help me know the difference. Amen.

Harsh or Gentle?

Sometimes we become angry and say things we are sorry about later. Put yourself in the situations below. With Proverbs 15:1 in mind, give your idea of what you could say—in a gentle way. Use the blank speech balloons to write your responses.

Your friend borrowed your favorite CD and   lost it. She tells you she's sorry and wonders   if you're mad.

Your younger brother is having trouble with his math. You've shown him how to do it three times, but he still doesn't get it and asks you to help him again.

Grandma got a very, very short haircut. You think she looks like she's joining the Marines. She asks you how you like it.

Dad brought home his favorite old movie and invites you to watch it with him. It bores you to tears, but he asks what you think of it.

Respectful

Respecting the flag is respecting the country for which it stands.

Show proper respect to everyone...honor the king.

~ 1 Peter 2:17

Proud Symbol

The soccer game between the Hartsville Hornets and the Midland Marvels was about to start. As the starting lineups were announced, Renae and her teammates ran out to be recognized.

"I wish we'd just start," she said to April. "I hate waiting around to play."

"We're going to be waiting a little longer," April responded as the band and color guard took their positions for the flag ceremony.

Everyone stood for the national anthem. More delay!

Might as well tie my shoe one more time, Renae thought as she bent down.

It was a rough and tumble game, but the Hornets won. The girls were whooping it up as they came to the bench after the game. Coach George asked them to sit down so he could talk to them.

"You played a great game," he said. "I'm proud of the way you worked together. Unfortunately, I'm not so proud of something else I observed."

The girls had puzzled looks on their faces. What was the coach talking about? They soon found out.

"Most of you were doing something else or doing nothing during the flag ceremony. The proper behavior is to place your hand over your heart, look at the flag and join in the national anthem," he explained. "When you do that, you are showing respect to our country's flag. The flag is a symbol of our country. So when you respect the flag you show respect to your country, its leaders and all the people who fought to give us the freedoms we have. Like the freedom to play soccer."

Your Turn

1. How do you show respect for your flag?

_____

_____

2. Why does God expect us to respect our country and its leaders?

_____

_____

Prayer

Lord, thank You for the freedoms our country enjoys. Help me respect our leaders and the flag. Amen.

 Researching the Flag

Your country's flag is so familiar that you hardly notice it or think about it. But it is the symbol of your country and there is a reason for each color and item on the flag. Do a little research in an encyclopedia or online to find out more about it. Then, look up some information on the Christian flag. You will probably find it quite interesting!

What do the symbols on your country's flag represent?

_____

_____

What do the colors stand for?

_____

_____

When was the first flag of your country made? What did it look like?

_____

_____

What are some ways people show respect to the flag?

_____

_____

What do the symbols on the Christian flag represent?

_____

_____

Name one interesting thing you discovered about the Christian flag.

_____

_____

Respectful

I should respect those in authority.

Obey your leaders...so that their work will be a joy, not a burden, for that would be of no advantage to you.

~ Hebrews 13:17

"R" is for Respect

The fifth-grade Sunday school class was waiting for their teacher, Mrs. Tober. They weren't exactly waiting quietly. Several boys were clowning around in front of the room, and everyone was talking and laughing.

Ramona said to Tami, "I wonder what happened to Mrs. Tober? She's never late."

Tami just grinned. "Hey, the longer she takes, the shorter the lesson. Let's play the name game." In this game, the players took turns thinking of descriptive words for a person for each letter in his or her name. Sometimes it was fun, but sometimes it was kind of mean when unkind things were said.

Three other girls joined Tami and Ramona. "Let's do Tober," Tami suggested.

Ramona suggested "timid," "tiny" and "talkative" for the letter "T." Then Tami said "O" with "out-of-style," which caused lots of laughing as the girls talked about Mrs. Tober's clothes.

"Boring" seemed to go well with the letter "B," they thought, and "easy" was paired with "E" because it was easy to get away with things in Mrs. Tober's class.

Tami poked Victoria. "You haven't said anything. How about "R"? Make it a good one!"

"How about 'respect'?" Victoria said. "Mrs. Tober shows respect to God and teaches us God's Word. So we should respect her. Respecting adults is the right thing to do, even if we don't like everything about them."

The girls were quiet as Mrs. Tober finally showed up.

Your Turn

1. Do you show respect to adult leaders? Why or why not?

_____

_____

2. How does showing respect for adults help you?

_____

_____

Prayer

Lord, show me how to be respectful to all the adults in my life. Amen.

 Expressing Your Respect

You probably have many adults, other than family, with whom you come in contact. They may be school teachers, coaches, Sunday school teachers or club leaders. How can you show respect for them and appreciation for what they do? Use one (or several) of these suggestions to brighten the day of one of the adults in your life.

Write a Note

Tell what you like about your leader and the class.

Send a Card

If you're not sure what to say, find a card that says "thank you" for you. Then write a short note and sign it.

Draw a Picture

If you can express yourself better by drawing than writing, go for it! Draw something you did together or something the person likes (cars, flowers, animals, etc.).

Tell Them

Tell the leaders "thanks" personally after a class or meeting.

Group Project

Get some of the other kids to work together on a group project. This could be a poster with pictures and notes, or a card signed by everyone. Give it to the leader on a special occasion, such as a birthday.

Respectful

I should show respect for older people.

Rise in the presence of the aged, show respect
for the elderly and revere your God.

~ Leviticus 19:32

Grandparents' Day

Mrs. Hartman passed out the monthly calendar just before dismissal.

"Something special has been added to the calendar this year," she said. "We are having a Grandparents' Day at the end of the month. Invite your grandparents to spend some time with us that day. It will be great to meet them, and maybe they can tell us what school was like when they were in fifth grade."

Christina, Monica and Jan walked home together. "Grandparents' Day sounds dumb to me," Monica said. "Why do we want to have a lot of old people at school? My grandpa doesn't even know how to use a computer."

"I know what you mean," Jan responded. "My grandparents are okay for old people–they're both in their 60s. Sometimes Gran tells me she doesn't think I 'dress properly' for school. What does she know about cool clothes?"

Christina was thinking about her Grandpa and Grandma Oliveri. She loved them but…Grandma had arthritis and had to use a cane. Grandpa had trouble hearing and even though he wore a hearing aid, he talked loudly. And Grandpa loved to talk–he was always telling jokes or stories. Neither one of them would win any fashion awards.

I can just imagine what Monica and Jan would think of my grandparents! Christina thought.

"I don't think I'm going to ask my mine," Jan said. "I'd be too embarrassed."

Monica nodded her head in agreement. Then she turned to Christina, "Hey, Chris. What about your grandparents? Gonna ask them to come?"

Your Turn

1. How do you feel about older people?

_____

_____

2. How can you show respect to them?

_____

_____

Prayer

God, help me to be respectful to older people. Amen.

Cookie Pops Bouquet

Many times older people live alone or they can't get out much and they feel lonely. Make a Cookie Pop Bouquet for an older person—maybe a neighbor, family member or someone from church. They will appreciate your thoughtfulness as much as the cookies.

What You Need

refrigerated cookie dough
rolling pin
cookie cutters
cookie sheet
craft sticks (¼" x 6")
frosting
baking decorations
wide ribbon
permanent marker
flower pot
foam block to fit pot

What to Do

1. Roll out dough to about ⅓"-½" thick.

2. Cut out shapes with cookie cutters

3. Place the cookies on the cookie sheet.

4. Carefully insert a craft stick into the bottom of each cookie.

5. Ask an adult to bake the cookies according to the package directions.

6. Meanwhile, cut the ribbon into 12" lengths.

7. Write a message or a Bible verse on each ribbon.

8. After the cookie pops cool, frost and decorate them.

9. Tie the ribbons around the craft sticks.

10. Place the foam in the bottom of the flower pot and stick the cookie pops in it to make a tasty bouquet.

Merciful

When I am merciful, I receive mercy.

Blessed are the merciful, for they will be shown mercy.

~ Matthew 5:7

Dina's Dilemma

Dina Cardova smiled to herself, amazed at what had happened. She had owed a dollar in library fines. After searching her pockets she found that she had forgotten her money at home. By the time she went home and returned, the library would have closed. She really needed to check out some books that day to write her report for school.

Just then, a teenage boy at the circulation desk had suddenly pulled a dollar out of his own pocket. He placed it into the fine box. "You can pay me back when you come in next time," he said.

As Dina left the library, she saw her uncle standing next to an empty parked car, getting ready to write a ticket. Her uncle was a traffic cop.

"Wait!" she heard someone yell from the window of the library. "I'll be out in a second." It was the teenage boy who had given her a dollar to pay her fine.

"Please don't give him a ticket!" Dina pleaded.

Her uncle looked up from his ticket book. "He didn't put money in the meter."

"Can't you wait until he comes out?"

Her uncle sighed, then agreed to wait. When the teenage boy ran out, with change in his hand, Dina's uncle shook his head. "You owe this young lady some thanks," he said to the boy.

The boy looked at Dina, then smiled.

Your Turn

1. How did the library employee receive mercy in return for his merciful act?

_____

_____

2. Have you ever received mercy instead of punishment? How did that make you feel?

_____

_____

Prayer

Lord Jesus, thank You for showing mercy to me. Amen.

A Time of Mercy

Use the first space below to write about a time when someone was merciful to you. Use the second space to describe how you can be merciful to someone. If you can't think of a way, use the space to write a prayer, asking God to help you be merciful.

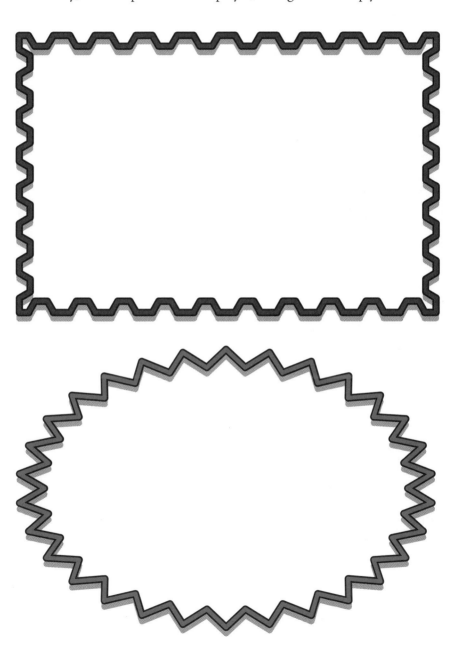

Merciful

God wants me to be merciful, even when I don't feel like it.

Be merciful, just as your Father is merciful.

~ Luke 6:36

Right Where I Want You

Anna Pippen smiled grimly. She had Devon Blaine right where she wanted her! When they were both in the fourth grade, Devon used to make fun of the way that Anna played volleyball. Over the summer, Anna had taken volleyball lessons at the Y. Now she was one of the best players in the fifth grade.

That's how she wound up being chosen in gym to be the captain of one of the volleyball teams. "You can pick who you want on your team," the gym teacher said.

Anna watched Devon squirm. Anna knew that Lisa, the other team captain, would not be in a hurry to choose Devon because Devon used to make fun of her, too. She knew Devon would be the last one chosen.

That would embarrass her for sure, Anna thought.

Suddenly the verse "Blessed are the merciful, for they will be shown mercy" (Matthew 5:7) popped into Anna's mind. She tried to ignore it as she opened her mouth to choose Staci for her team. But she couldn't as she looked at Devon's miserable face.

With a sigh, Anna said, "Devon."

Devon's look was grateful as she ran to join Anna's team.

Your Turn

1. How did Anna show mercy toward Devon?

_____

_____

2. What would you have done if you were Anna? Why?

_____

_____

3. Why do you think God wants us to show mercy toward others?

_____

_____

Prayer

God, I don't always feel like being merciful. Please show me ways to be merciful, even when I don't feel like it. Amen.

A Call for Mercy?

Look at the scene below. Does this situation call for mercy? Use the empty speech balloon to write a response that shows mercy. Draw yourself below that balloon!

Merciful

**God is merciful when He doesn't give
me the punishment I deserve.**

*But the wisdom that comes from heaven is
first of all pure; then...full of mercy.*

~ James 3:17

Wanted: Tara Purcell

Tara Purcell knew she was in trouble. She didn't have to guess when she saw the expression on her mother's face.

So what if I'm a little late coming home from Steph's house? she reasoned.

She glanced at her mother's face again.

Okay, a lot late. Two hours late. I'm gonna be grounded for sure. Or at least I'll get "the talk."

Mrs. Purcell folded her arms. "You know we taught you how to tell time," she began.

Tara almost laughed at that. "I'm sorry I'm late, Mom. I know I was supposed to be home at 3:30. I...lost track of the time."

Mrs. Purcell pursed her lips. "Hmm. What should I do with you now?"

"Give me a kiss?" Tara grinned.

Mrs. Purcell suddenly caught her daughter in a hug. "I'm feeling merciful today. I will give you that kiss." She kissed Tara's forehead.

Tara was more surprised than she had been in a long time.

"Next time, come home when I tell you. I don't make rules just to hear myself talk. I want you to be safe, Tara."

Your Turn

1. What did Tara receive instead of what she deserved?

_____

_____

2. How would you have felt had you been Tara? Why?

_____

_____

Prayer

Father God, thanks to Jesus, I won't receive the punishment my sins deserve. Thank You for Your mercy. Amen.

A Word from Our Sponsor

An Old Testament prophet named Zechariah had an important message from God for the people of Israel. That message is for you, too. Use the sign language code to figure out the letter each sign represents and write the letter on the line.

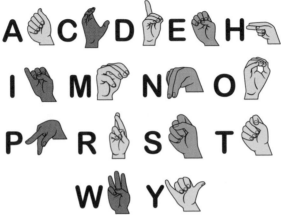

A C D E H
I M N O
P R S T
W Y

The solution is on page 235.

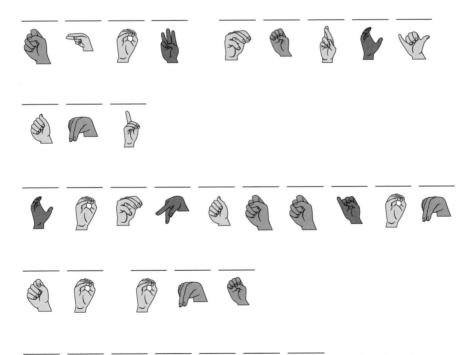

~ Zechariah 7:9

Unselfish

Being unselfish means putting others first.

*For I have come down from heaven not to do my will
but to do the will of him who sent me.*

~ John 6:38

Mrs. Rice

As Deborah Walls walked into the house, she was mad enough to shoot flames. "Mrs. Rice made us move again!" she complained to her mother.

"Deb, you know she doesn't like you and your friends to hang out in front of her house," Mrs. Walls said.

Deborah fingered her strawberry-blond ponytail. "Mom, I thought the park bench was public property!"

"Yes, but it's in front of her house." Mrs. Walls smiled. "And Deb, you do tend to attract a lot of kids."

"I can't help that, Mom!" Deborah made friends easily. Many of her friends had come to know Jesus because of her. "Anyway, it's not fair!"

"Deb, don't forget Mrs. Rice lost a daughter who would've been in sixth grade like you are now. I think…seeing you around reminds her of what she lost."

Deborah thought about that.

"So, WWJD?" Mrs. Walls said with a grin.

"Huh?" Deborah asked.

"What would Jesus do in this situation?"

"I'm not the one who's selfish!"

"Deborah."

"Okay, okay! Maybe I can get my friends to hang out someplace else." She paused. "Maybe I could also make Mrs. Rice some cookies or something."

"I think she'd like that."

Your Turn

1. How was Deborah encouraged to be unselfish?

_____

_____

2. How would you respond to Mrs. Rice? Why?

_____

_____

Prayer

Lord, being unselfish is hard sometimes. Please help me to think of others, even when I don't want to do it.

Something to Keep in Mind

Want to be unselfish? Then remember 2 Corinthians 2:16. Don't know the verse? Then put the letters below each column in the boxes above that column. The letters may not be listed in the exact order in which they appear in the quote. Mark off used letters at the bottom. A letter may only be used once. The black boxes stand for the end of a word.

The solution is on page 235.

113

Unselfish

Selfishness and love don't mix.

[Love] is not rude, it is not self-seeking, it is not easily angered.

~ 1 Corinthians 13:5

Unselfish Erin

Erin wasn't selfish–no not one bit.
Just ask her little brother: the little twit.
(That was Erin's opinion, when she was mad.
She was often angry with her brother, Brad.)

Unlike Brad, she was always good.
She did everything right as best as she could.
She shared her toys, at least the ones she
didn't like.
Why, she'd even given away her least
favorite bike!

When Brad asked to watch his favorite show
On TV that night, Erin didn't say no.
Instead she made him quickly agree
To do a chore for her…or two or three.

Well, it was her night to pick the show.
As she reminded him, just so he'd know.
Yes, Erin wasn't selfish–no, not one bit.
Just ask her little brother, the little twit.

Your Turn

1. Take a look at the Scripture above. What advice would you have for Erin?

_____

_____

2. Based on the Scripture, what advice would you have for yourself?

_____

_____

Prayer

Lord, when I'm tempted to be selfish, please remind me to be kind. Amen.

Free Advice

Here is some advice for Erin and for you about being unselfish. Start at the letter at the arrow. Skip every other letter in two trips around the circle. Print the letters on the lines at the bottom. (As you go around the circle the second time, skip the first letter that you used.) The solution is on page 235.

_____

_____

Unselfish

I should be unselfish because it is the right
thing to do, not just to make a good impression.

Don't be selfish; don't live to make a good impression on others.

Philippians 2:3 NLT

An Unselfish Example

Martina Jane Edwards–Student Leader of the Year!

Marti could almost hear the principal call out her name in assembly. In her mind's eye, she pictured herself strolling to the stage and accepting a big plaque.

All of the teachers had complimented Marti. "Oh, Martina is so helpful," she remembered hearing her fifth-grade teacher, Mr. Webb, say to her mother at the close of the school band concert.

"Marti! I need some help to clean the garage," her brother, Doug, suddenly called from her bedroom doorway, interrupting her daydream. "Can you help me?"

"I'm busy!" Marti called, as she relaxed on her bed. "Ask Caitlin!"

Yes, Marti thought as she returned to her daydream, *my teachers are right to think I'm helpful.*

"Marti, could you help me with my art project?" her brother, Raymond, called from his room.

"I'm busy!" Marti yelled.

Marti went back to her daydream. *I can't wait for that assembly,* she thought. *I'm sure my helpfulness will win me that award.*

Your Turn

1. Would Marti's brothers describe her as unselfish? Why or why not?

_____

_____

2. How would your friends or family describe you?

_____

_____

Prayer

Lord, I want to be unselfish like You are, not to try to make a good impression on others. Amen.

Ways to Be Unselfish

Unscramble the words below to find ways to be unselfish.

The solution is on page 235.

JUST A NOTE...

Do a HEROC for someone.

YARP for someone.

VOLE others.

Be TEGLEN.

Give ITEM to ELPH someone.

Caring

I can care for all types of people.

There should be no division in the body…its parts should have equal concern for each other. If one part suffers, every part suffers with it; if one part is honored, every part rejoices with it.

1 Corinthians 12:25-26

Wesley Street Church

Heather Billek couldn't help being curious after hearing her mother say, "How terrible!" several times.

"What's terrible?" she asked after her mother hung up the phone.

"Wesley Street Church had a fire in its Sunday school wing yesterday."

Heather grabbed an apple from a nearby bowl. "I thought we didn't like that church," she said.

Mrs. Billek threw her a look. "Just because we don't worship together doesn't mean we don't care about each other."

Heather remembered the conversation they had had the previous year. Her church and Wesley Street Church used to be one church. Because of a big argument, some of the members of Heather's church left to form the Wesley Street Church.

"I still don't understand why we're not all still the same church," Heather said.

"Well, we don't always get along together. But when we do disagree and something bad happens, we can still care for each other."

Your Turn

1. Do you have to like someone in order to care about that person? Why or why not?

_____

_____

2. Is there someone you know for whom you have difficulty caring? Why? Use the prayer below to be honest with God.

_____

_____

Prayer

God, You know I have trouble caring about _____ . Help me, Lord, to show concern for this person. Amen.

Your Definition

What's your definition of "caring"? Use words that describe actions beginning with each letter. For example, "C" could stand for "concern for others."

C _____

A _____

R _____

I _____

N _____

G _____

Caring

I can show my concern for others by helping them.

Carry each other's burdens, and in this way you will fulfill the law of Christ.

~ Galatians 6:2

Let Me Carry Them!

"Why do you keep trying to carry my backpack?" Steve Fletcher asked as he paused in the middle of the sidewalk in front of the middle school.

Mindy Gerard almost giggled as she saw the annoyed look on her friend's sunburned face. "I'm trying to carry your burdens," she said as she yanked the bag's strap from his shoulder. He almost fell over.

"My what?" The look on Steve's face changed to a puzzled one.

"Your burdens," Mindy patiently explained. "That means I'm supposed to care about you, ya dope. Now let me carry your backpack to the bus stop."

Steve turned to look at the bus stop. "Wow. A whole 10 feet from here. Gee, thanks."

He turned back to Mindy. "So, when I asked you to help me figure out my algebra homework yesterday, how come you didn't want to help if you're so concerned?"

Mindy laughed. "I'd rather just carry your backpack."

"Oh," laughed Steve. "So you are a 'selective' burden carrier?"

Your Turn

1. Do you think Mindy really cared about Steve? Why or why not?

_____

_____

2. Does caring for others only mean caring about some of the things they care about? Why or why not?

_____

_____

3. How will you carry someone's burdens this week?

_____

_____

Prayer

Lord, show me how to carry others' burdens at home, school and church. Amen.

Your Brand of Caring

You see advertisements everywhere. Suppose you could put an advertising slogan on the backpack or notebook you carry around. What slogan would you use to tell people about the importance of caring for others? Let the sample backpack inspire you, then write your own on the blank one.

Caring

God wants me to care for my enemies as well as my friends.

*Dear children, let us not love with words or
tongue but with actions and in truth.*

~ 1 John 3:18

The Meanest Person in the World?

Lizzie Shriver stopped when she heard her friend, Daria Wilson, call her name. Daria ran to catch up with her.

"What's that?" Daria asked, pointing to the purple, plastic-covered dish in Lizzie's hand.

"Cupcakes. Gotta deliver 'em," Lizzie said.

"I'll walk with you."

As the two girls walked down the block, Daria soon pointed to a green house toward the end. An older man sat on the porch. "Hmmph. I see Mr. Walker's on his porch," she said. "He never says anything nice to anyone. I'll bet he's the meanest person in the world."

Lizzie didn't answer at first. "When my dad died last year, Mrs. Walker brought us groceries. Mr. Walker cut our lawn every week in the summer and drove Brandon and me to soccer practice whenever Mom couldn't." She bit her lip, having said more than she normally said.

As Lizzie marched up to the porch alone and handed Mr. Walker the cupcakes, Daria watched with surprise.

Your Turn

1. How did Lizzie show concern for the Walkers?

_____

_____

2. Do you think Mr. Walker is the way Daria thinks he is? Why or why not?

_____

_____

Prayer

Lord, may my words and actions be the same as I show love to others. Amen.

Brooke's Day

Meet Brooke. You're invited to go through one day in her life. Your job is to help her be more concerned for others. Start at 7:30 a.m. and move clockwise. End at 7:30 p.m. Each entry shows one of Brooke's actions. You can play by yourself or with a friend. Use a penny to move. Heads, you move up one hour; tails, you go back one hour. If you land on a space where Brooke does something uncaring, you'll have to remain there one turn unless you can name a caring thing Brooke could do. If you land on a free hour, skip ahead one space. If you play with a friend, flip a coin to see who goes first. (Tails goes first!) Play until you cannot think of any more caring things to do!

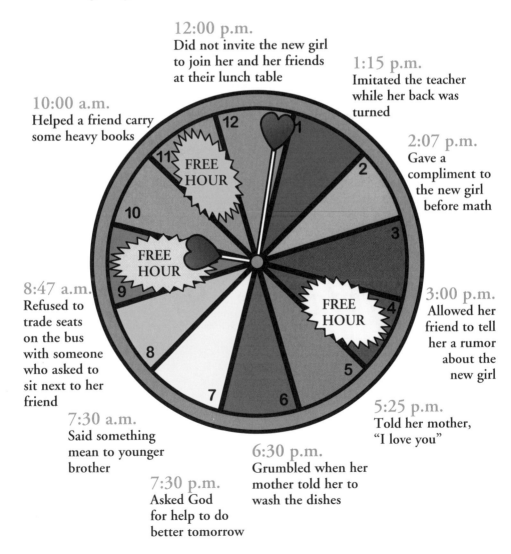

12:00 p.m.
Did not invite the new girl to join her and her friends at their lunch table

1:15 p.m.
Imitated the teacher while her back was turned

10:00 a.m.
Helped a friend carry some heavy books

2:07 p.m.
Gave a compliment to the new girl before math

8:47 a.m.
Refused to trade seats on the bus with someone who asked to sit next to her friend

3:00 p.m.
Allowed her friend to tell her a rumor about the new girl

7:30 a.m.
Said something mean to younger brother

5:25 p.m.
Told her mother, "I love you"

6:30 p.m.
Grumbled when her mother told her to wash the dishes

7:30 p.m.
Asked God for help to do better tomorrow

123

Cooperative

God wants me to cooperate with others.

How good and pleasant it is when brothers live together in unity!

~ Psalm 133:1

The TV Blowup

Lili raced to the family room, turned on the TV and grabbed the remote. Denzel followed her and gave a loud groan when he saw what Lili was watching.

"Yuck! Who wants to watch this dumb show?" he wailed.

"Me," answered Lili.

Denzel flopped on the floor, making horrible gagging sounds. "It's my turn to choose what to watch," he argued. "And I want to see the basketball game!"

Lili said, "No way! And I have the remote!"

"Dad!" yelled Denzel. "Lili's hogging the TV!"

Mr. Barth didn't look very happy as he came through the door. He turned off the TV and motioned for Lili to give him the remote. The remote went into his pocket. He folded his arms over his chest.

"Watching TV is not a competitive sport with a winner," their dad said. "It should be a matter of cooperation. Taking turns makes everyone happier–the people involved and God. God wants us to live peacefully with each other."

Mr. Barth continued, "TV watching is off limits for three days. During that time, we'll work out a cooperative plan for taking turns in choosing programs."

Lili and Denzel agreed. Cooperation sounded better than fighting. And maybe, just maybe, they might like each other's programs.

Your Turn

1. What do you and the other kids in your family fight about?

_____

_____

2. How can all of you cooperate to make things more peaceful?

_____

_____

Prayer

God of peace, help me to live in harmony with my family. Amen.

Working Together

Cooperation means working together with other people to do something. Many groups need to cooperate in order to accomplish what needs to be done. Decode the words below to find out who some of these groups are. Then write your family name on the blank line. The solution is on page 236.

Cooperation Code

1=N 2=S 3=E 4=R 5=Y 6=H 7=C 8=F 9=A 10=G

11=T 12=I 13=D 14=P 15=L 16=B 17=O 18=U 19=M

```
‾‾ ‾‾ ‾‾ ‾‾
16  9  1  13
```

```
‾‾ ‾‾ ‾‾ ‾‾ ‾‾        ‾‾ ‾‾ ‾‾ ‾‾ ‾‾
2  14  17  4  11      11  3  9  19  2
```

```
‾‾ ‾‾ ‾‾ ‾‾
9   4  19  5
```

```
‾‾ ‾‾ ‾‾ ‾‾ ‾‾ ‾‾        ‾‾ ‾‾ ‾‾ ‾‾ ‾‾ ‾‾
7  6  18  4  7  6        8  9  19  12  15  5
```

```
‾‾ ‾‾ ‾‾ ‾‾ ‾‾ ‾‾ ‾‾ ‾‾ ‾‾
17  4  7  6  3  2  11  4  9
```

```
‾‾ ‾‾ ‾‾ ‾‾        ‾‾ ‾‾ ‾‾ ‾‾ ‾‾ ‾‾ ‾‾ ‾‾
8  12  4  3        8  12  10  6  11  3  4  2
```

```
‾‾ ‾‾ ‾‾ ‾‾ ‾‾ ‾‾ ‾‾ ‾‾ ‾‾ ‾‾
7  15  9  2  2  19  9  11  3  2
```

```
‾‾ ‾‾ ‾‾ ‾‾        ‾‾ ‾‾ ‾‾ ‾‾ ‾‾ ‾‾ ‾‾ ‾‾
6  17  19  3        16  18  12  15  13  3  4  2
```

The _____ family.

Cooperative

Family cooperation helps everyone.

Carry each other's burdens, and in this way you will fulfill the law of Christ.

~ Galatians 6:2

Read It Again

Laura was talking to Jennifer on the phone as her mother and sister came in the door. Three-year-old Sophie was whining and fussing. "I want my kitty book!" she wailed. "I don't want to take off my coat! I just want my book!"

As she took off her coat, Mrs. Simons looked at Laura. "Please get off the phone," she said. "You need to entertain Sophie while I fix dinner."

Laura frowned and said to Jennifer, "I have to say good-bye. My whiny sister is driving Mom nuts and I guess I need to read to her. See ya."

"Why do I have to entertain Sophie?" Laura complained. "She can play by herself."

Then Laura noticed that Mom looked really tired. Sophie was still sniffling, but at least she had taken off her coat. Laura looked at Sophie with her little arms folded over her chest just waiting to see what was going to happen.

"Oh, alright, Sophie," Laura sighed. "Go get your kitty book."

"Yea!" squealed Sophie as she raced to the bookshelf. Mrs. Simons smiled at Laura and gave her a "thumbs-up" sign.

Maybe I'll only have to read about Katie Kitty four times today, thought Laura.

Your Turn

1. Why is it important for a family to cooperate?

_____

_____

2. What are some ways you can help your family by being cooperative? Will it be easy for you? Why or why not?

_____

_____

Prayer

Heavenly Father, thank You for putting me in a family. Help me to be cooperative. Amen.

Godly Appeal

Figure out the clues and then write the answers on the numbered blanks. The message will offer you some good advice about being cooperative.

____ _____ _____ _____ ... _____ _____
  1   5   4   12   11   3

____ _____ _____ _____ _____
  7   12   6   8   2

_____ . _____ _____ : ____
      10   13   2   9

1. How you refer to yourself

2. First number

3. Everyone or everything

4. Opposite of "from"

5. "Ap" + what a bell does (rhymes with "real")

6. Think the same way (rhymes with "tree")

7. Remove the first and last letter of "soft"

8. Add a "w" to the front of "it" and an "h" to the end

9. Number of disciples minus two

10. Add an "a" to the front of "not" and "her" to the end

11. Doing this and _____ (rhymes with "cat")

12. Opposite of "me"

13. Seventh book of the New Testament

The solution is on page 236.

Cooperative

I can accomplish more if I cooperate.

Whatever you do, whether in word or deed, do it all in the name of the Lord Jesus, giving thanks to God the Father through him.

~ Colossians 3:17

The Talent Fair

The kids at Madison Middle School were getting ready for the annual Talent Fair. The fair was a big event with parents, grandparents, neighbors and other interested people attending.

Mrs. Stone announced to the fifth-graders, "Our class has been asked to make posters advertising the Talent Fair. They will be put up all around school and in the stores downtown. You can work on them during art periods for the next two weeks." She then divided the class into groups of three, with each group responsible for two posters. Alexandria, Beth and Allen were in one group.

Mrs. Stone gave them the information and materials they needed. She stressed that they really needed to get busy and couldn't waste time.

"I've made posters before," Beth said importantly. "So I know what to do."

"Well, who died and made you boss?" Allen snarled as he grabbed a piece of poster board and some markers.

Alexandria just leaned back in her chair. "I don't care who's boss. I can't draw anyway."

Mrs. Stone had been watching and listening. Now she came over and said, "This is called a Talent Fair because everyone does something he or she is good at. It also means everyone needs to cooperate to make it successful. The same thing is true of making posters. Think about it."

Your Turn

1. How could the group cooperate to make the posters?

_____

_____

2. Do you think other people consider you to be a cooperative person? If not, how can you start to develop a spirit of cooperation?

_____

_____

Prayer

Lord, show me ways to cooperate with others, like Jesus did. Amen.

 # Working for God

To remind you of the memory verse on page 128, search for the highlighted words in the puzzle below. The solution is on page 236.

Whatever you do, whether in word or deed,
do it all in the name of the Lord Jesus,
giving thanks to God the Father through him.

~ Colossians 3:17

S	K	N	A	H	T	W	O	R	D
T	R	J	E	N	A	H	N	D	E
H	E	W	H	A	T	E	V	E	R
R	H	L	T	M	T	T	E	E	A
O	T	L	R	E	L	H	E	D	N
U	A	A	S	U	S	E	J	E	D
G	F	A	G	O	D	R	O	L	L
H	I	M	L	W	U	O	Y	O	W

Forgiving

I should forgive my enemies.

Be kind and compassionate to one another, forgiving each other, just as in Christ God forgave you.

~ Ephesians 4:32

Forgiving the Enemy

The Bakers were on their way to the veterans' home where Uncle Willie lived. Paris didn't really want to go, but 8-year-old Eric was excited about talking to a "real" soldier.

After greeting her great-uncle, Paris kind of melted into the background and kept quiet. But there was nothing shy about Eric. He stared at Uncle Willie's hand and blurted out, "Why do you have such a weird hand?"

Uncle Willie just laughed. "Well, boy, this is a fake arm and hand. So's my leg. Left the real ones in a prison camp across the ocean."

"Wow!" said Eric. "What happened?" Paris even leaned forward to hear the answer.

Uncle Willie had a faraway look in his eyes as he said, "I was scouting for my unit when I walked into an ambush. I was shot up pretty bad and then taken to the enemy's camp. They didn't have a very good doctor, so I lost my leg and arm. Stayed in that prison camp for three years–until the end of the war."

Paris said, "You must have absolutely hated those enemy soldiers."

"At first I really did hate them," Uncle Willie said. "But I had lots of time to think about things and I remembered Bible stories and verses I had learned. I also prayed a lot. I decided that if Jesus could forgive the men who were crucifying Him, I sure could forgive these enemy soldiers. I even started praying for them."

Paris moved closer. She wanted to know more about this forgiveness.

Your Turn

1. Why did Uncle Willie forgive the enemies?

_____

_____

2. Are we supposed to forgive people only when they ask to be forgiven? Why or why not?

_____

_____

Prayer

Dear Jesus, help me to forgive others, just as You forgive me. Amen.

True Forgiveness

Jesus died on the cross so that the sins of all people could be forgiven. He did this out of love. To find out what Jesus prayed for the people who crucified Him, fill in the boxes using the code:

@ - A	^ - M
# - D	$ - N
☀ - E	••➤ - O
ℭ - F	? - R
+ - G	< - T
■ - H	> - V
✝ - I	X - W
♣ - K	✪ - Y

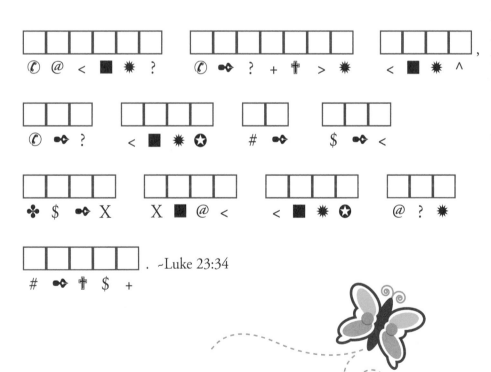

ℭ @ < ■ ☀ ?   ℭ ••➤ ? + ✝ > ☀   < ■ ☀ ^ ,

ℭ ••➤ ?   < ■ ☀ ✪   # ••➤ $ ••➤ <

♣ $ ••➤ X   X ■ @ <   < ■ ☀ ✪   @ ? ☀

••➤ ✝ $ + . ~Luke 23:34

The solution is on page 236.

Forgiving

I should forgive my friends.

Forgive us our sins, for we also forgive everyone who sins against us.

~ Luke 11:4

The Lie

Mr. Loy watched as his daughter, Kim, came into the family bookstore. Her feet were dragging and her head was down as she came through the door.

"I can see you had a bad day," said her father.

"Worse than bad. Horrible. Terrible." Kim threw her backpack on the counter, almost knocking over the stack of books on it.

"Want to talk about it?" Mr. Loy asked.

Kim let out a big sigh and plopped onto a stool. She explained how her friend Natalie had told a lie about her. Natalie had lied to avoid getting in trouble for something she had done. The principal found out the truth and called Natalie to the office.

"It hurts a lot when someone lies about you, especially a friend," her father sympathized.

Kim nodded. "Natalie told me she was sorry. But I don't know if I can forgive her for what she did."

"It can be hard, but Jesus said we are to forgive others just as He forgives us. If you can't do it, Jesus will help you. Why don't we pray about it right now?"

Your Turn

1. Why do you think Kim had a hard time forgiving Natalie?

_____

_____

2. When have you found it difficult to forgive someone? What did you do?

_____

_____

Prayer

Lord, thank You for forgiving me. Help me to forgive others in the same way. Amen.

Forgiveness Formula

Fill in the blanks to find the true forgiveness formula.

1. Read Colossians 3:13. How are you to forgive?

_____

2. Read Mark 11:25. Who are you to forgive?

_____

3. Read Matthew 6:12. Why should you forgive someone?

_____

4. Read Luke 17:4. How many times should you forgive someone?

_____

I, _____, have sin in my life. God _____

_____ me because of Jesus' death and resurrection. Now I

can _____ others.

The solution is on page 236.

Forgiving

I should forgive others as Jesus forgives me.

If he sins against you seven times in a day, and seven times comes back to you and says, "I repent," forgive him.

~ Luke 17:4

Forgiving Joe

Nola had a brother named Joe.
He never listened when she said "No!"
Joe got into Nola's room and all of her things,
Her books, her games and even her earrings.
One day everything was in a heap on her floor.
Nola screamed, "Get out!" and slammed the door.
"I'm sorry," Joe wailed out in the hall.
Nola didn't think he meant it at all.
"Will you forgive me?" asked Joe.
"You're not really sorry. So, no."
Their mom heard everything they said.
She came in the door, shaking her head.
"I know you're angry with Joe for this mess
But you can't deny him your forgiveness.
Jesus forgives all your sins every day
He expects you to treat others in the same way."
Nola half-smiled at Joe and said, "OK."
He grinned back and helped her put things away.

Your Turn

1. Did Nola have the right to not forgive Joe? Why or why not?

_____

_____

2. Has someone ever told you he or she would not forgive you? How did you feel?

_____

_____

Prayer

Lord, sometimes I don't want to forgive. I need Your help to be forgiving. Amen.

Forgiveness Flowers

Make some flower bouquets to use for forgiveness.

What You Need

colored construction paper
scissors
glue
markers
crayons
glitter
craft sticks
cup or small can

What to Do

1. Cut colored construction paper into strips, circles, triangles and other shapes.

2. Glue the shapes together to make different kinds of flowers. You can decorate the flowers with markers, crayons or glitter.

3. Tape or glue a craft stick to the back of each flower for the stem.

4. On each stem write a message, such as "God loves you" or "You are forgiven" or "Let's be friends."

5. Put the flowers into a pretty cup or decorated can. Whenever you fight with someone, give a flower to the person with whom you argued. This will let the person know that you forgive him or her.

Kind

I can show God's kindness toward others.

*Be kind and compassionate to one another, forgiving
each other, just as in Christ God forgave you.*

~ Ephesians 4:32

Christina's Diary

Today at school, Weird Clarence told me that he forgave me. Just like that. Well, after he heard me at school telling Tai and Syreeta about how uncool he dresses sometimes. I didn't know he was around the corner! I felt terrible, but everybody thinks that. That's why he has the name Weird Clarence.

Even after hearing me say that, he loaned me money at lunchtime to buy milk after I found that I had lost the money Mom gave me.

Syreeta said, "I think Clarence likes you." But I don't think that. Neither does Tai. I think Clarence is just...nice. I've heard other kids say that, even the ones who call him weird. He once told me that he's a Christian. Mom says she doesn't believe in God. But I think there is a God. Clarence's kindness proves that.

Maybe I should stop calling him Weird Clarence?

Your Turn

1. How did Clarence show kindness to Christina?

_____

_____

2. What does Christina think about God, based on Clarence's example?

_____

_____

3. Who is the kindest person you know? Why did you choose this person?

_____

_____

Prayer

God, I want to have the same kind heart that Jesus has. Amen.

Advice from 1st Thessalonians

To get some advice on kindness from God's Word, unscramble the letters to make the words. Then unscramble the words to put them in the correct order.

The solution is on page 236.

grown ot ruse sayp trohe rof rowng tub to roveryene eb

ot atth heac selonasiathans dink dan donoby kame slee.

1 swayl ryt 5:15 cabk

_____

_____

Kind

I can show kindness by standing up for a friend.

A kind man benefits himself, but a cruel man brings trouble on himself.

~ Proverbs 11:17

The Note

"Get away from her!"

That was all Danielle Owen could think to say after seeing the note taped to her friend's backpack while they waited for the school bus. The note had one word: "Chubbo."

Danielle had caught two seventh-graders—Jason and his friend, Eddie—in the act of leaving the note. She knew they liked to tease kids in the sixth grade. They had locked on to Michaela that week. Every so often they would make loud comments about her weight.

Danielle snatched the note off the backpack, thankful that Michaela hadn't seen it. Michaela was still getting water at the drinking fountain. She couldn't bear to see a hurt look on Michaela's face.

Just as she started to ball up the note, a hand touched her shoulder.

"I'll take that," the vice principal, Mr. Hathaway, said.

Danielle almost jumped. She hadn't realized that he stood near. "But I didn't..."

"Don't worry. I know the culprits. They've been causing trouble all week." He went back inside the school.

Danielle shook her head. The look on Mr. Hathaway's face told her that Jason and Eddie were in trouble. She was glad not to be in their shoes!

Your Turn

1. What would you have done?

_____

_____

2. One of the kindest acts you can do is to stand up for a friend. Have you ever done that? What happened as a result?

_____

_____

Prayer

Lord, help me to act kindly to those who have suffered the cruelty of others. Amen.

Kindness Clues

Feeling clueless about kindness? Help is on the way. For this puzzle, you'll need an NIV Bible.

The first two words of Psalm 23:1

The eighth word in Genesis 22:14

The sixteenth word in John 14:26

The second word in Romans 7:1

The eleventh and twelfth words in Matthew 4:1

The second word in Proverbs 11:17.

_____

_____

The solution is on page 236.

Kind

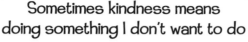

Sometimes kindness means doing something I don't want to do

The Lord's servant must not quarrel; instead, he must be kind to everyone.

~ 2 Timothy 2:24

Quinn's Request

"So, will you take out the garbage for me?" Quinn asked his younger sister, Rachel. "It needs to be taken out before Dad gets home. But I don't have time right now. Pedro and his dad are out in the car waiting for me."

Rachel thought about Quinn's request for a second. She knew he didn't want to keep Pedro and his father waiting. They were almost late for karate practice. But she was sick of doing favors for him. What was she, the maid?

"No," she said, just as she heard the horn blow.

"Please," Quinn begged. "I'll wash the dishes for you tomorrow night."

"Won't work this time," Rachel decided.

Quinn looked disgusted. "Great. Dad's gonna kill me." He ran out the door.

Rachel grinned as she slipped on the earphones to her portable CD player. Her favorite Christian music group sang about Jesus' kindness. Jesus had willingly come to do the Father's will.

As she listened, she couldn't help feeling a little guilty about the way that she treated Quinn. Sure, he was a pest, always wanting a favor. But she knew that was no excuse not to help him.

So with a sigh, she got up and took out the garbage.

Your Turn

1. What unselfish act inspired Rachel? Why?

_____

_____

2. What does that act inspire you to do? Why?

_____

_____

Prayer

Jesus, thank You for Your kindness. Amen.

Kindness Ingredients

Good cooks know how to follow a recipe. Kind people do, too. Did you know there is a "recipe" for kindness? It can be found in 2 Peter 1:5-7. Use the code to find out the ingredients for kindness.

A	B	C	D	E	F	G	H	I	J	K
✡	✜	✛	✤	✦	◆	✧	★	☆	✪	✩

L	N	O	P	R	S	T	U	V	W	Y
★	★	☆	☆	✻	✳	✲	✴	✶	✷	✸

Add to your faith _____

✧ ✲ ✻ ✤ ✻ ✦ ✳ ✴

and to goodness, _____ ;

✪ ★ ★ ✴ ★ ✤ ✤ ✧ ✤

and to knowledge, _____ _____;

✳ ✤ ★ ◆   ✛ ✪ ★ ★ ✻ ★ ✪

and to self-control, _____;

☆ ✤ ✳ ✴ ✤ ✴ ✤ ✻ ✡ ★ ✛ ✤

and to perseverance, _____;

✧ ✲ ✤ ★ ✪ ★ ✤ ✴ ✳

and to godliness, _____   _____;

✜ ✻ ✪ ✴ ★ ✤ ✻ ★ ✸   ✪ ✪ ★ ✤ ★ ✤ ✴ ✳

and to brotherly kindness, _____.

✪ ★ ✲ ✤

~ 2 Peter 1:5-7

The solution is on page 236.

Fair

God wants me to show fairness in my actions.

[Do] what is right and just and fair.

~ Proverbs 1:3

It's Not Fair!

"What's wrong?"

What's right? Molly Larson wanted to say in answer to her father's question. She was glad to see he was home early when she came home that afternoon after school. She sniffed the air. At least he was making lasagna. That was the only thing right about that day.

"I wanted to be on the sixth-grade party-planning committee, but Mrs. Douglas picked Allison. She always picks her for everything. Just because her dad owns everything in town. It's not fair!" Molly paused for breath. "And what's worse, Allison's been assigned to my math study group. We're supposed to help each other. Well, I'm not gonna help her."

Her father didn't say anything for a few moments. "Need a hug, Mol?" he finally asked.

Molly nodded, trying to fight back angry tears. "Daddy, I don't wanna help Allison," she said against his sweater.

Mr. Larson smoothed her hair. "I know it's not fair, but I know you'll do the right thing."

"And what's that?"

"What God wants you to do."

Your Turn

1. What do you think Molly should do?

_____

_____

2. What would you do in this situation?

_____

_____

Prayer

Jesus, sometimes life isn't fair! When it isn't, help me to obey You anyway. Amen.

What's Right and Fair?

Take a look at the Scripture on page 142. What will you do this week to do "what is right and just and fair"? Use the space below to describe or draw a picture of one thing you can do.

Fair

God wants me to be fair to all people, even my enemies.

Do not show partiality in judging; hear both small and great alike.

~ Deuteronomy 1:17

Kris's Choice

Kris Walters watched the volleyball sail over the net. If it went out of bounds, her team would win.

The ball looked very close to the out-of-bounds line.

"Out!" Jasmine Meyer, Kris's teammate and best friend, called.

"Whadddya mean 'out'? It was in!" a boy on the other team yelled.

"Out!" Jasmine yelled.

"In!"

The gym teacher's whistle soon ended the argument. "Kris, you were closest," he said. "Was the ball in or out?"

Kris paused before answering. The person who had served the ball was someone she didn't really like. Yet, she had to admit that the ball was within the line.

I could still say it was out, Kris thought. She glanced at her best friend. She seemed to silently plead with her to say the ball was out.

Your Turn

1. What would be the fair choice for Kris? Why?

_____

_____

2. Should you be fair only to the people you like? Why or why not?

_____

_____

3. What do you usually do when you're faced with making a fair choice?

_____

_____

Prayer

Father God, I'm not always sure how to be fair. Please remind me, through the Holy Spirit, when I need to be fair. Amen.

A Fairness First Step

When you want to make a fair choice, here's the first step. Make a copy of the puzzle below, then cut out the pieces and put them together to find out what it is.

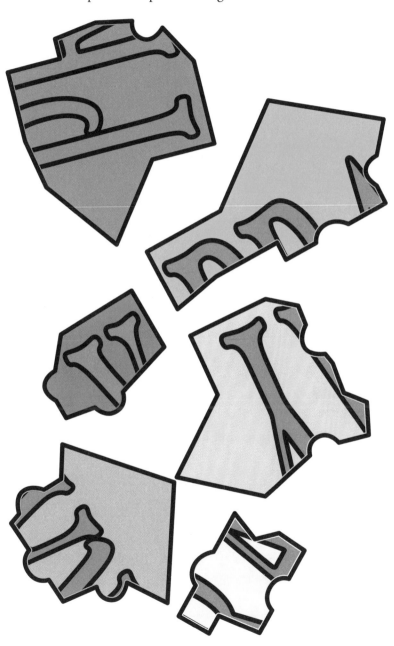

The solution is on page 236.

Fair

I can be fair as Jesus was.

Do to others as you would have them do to you.

~ Luke 6:31

Equal Share?

"One for you." Megan Lewis handed her six-year-old sister one chocolate chip cookie. "And three for me."

Samantha stared at the one cookie. "Hey! You got more than I got."

"That's because I'm older than you. Besides, Mom said I could pass them out."

"But that's not fair!" Samantha's bottom lip quivered and her blue eyes filled with tears.

Megan shrugged. "When you get to fifth grade in four years, you can have more."

"Moooooom! Megan only gave me one cookie!"

"You big tattle-tale!"

"I don't want to hear any fighting!" their mother called from her bedroom.

"Oh, here!" Megan practically threw a cookie at her sister. "I was only teasing." She knew she hadn't been.

Samantha took the cookie, then pointed to Megan's bracelet. The letters WWJD could be seen. "What does that mean again?"

Megan didn't want to admit it. "What would Jesus do."

"I don't think Jesus would've done what you did." She stuck out her tongue, then ran off.

Megan started to run after her, but stopped. She couldn't help thinking about what her sister said.

Your Turn

1. Of what did Samantha remind her? How do you think that would help Megan?

_____

_____

2. Suppose you were Megan. What would you have done differently?

_____

Prayer

God, help me not to make excuses, especially when it comes to being fair. Amen.

 Who Deserves Fairness?

Does everyone deserve to be treated fairly? Look at the list of people below. Decide who deserves fair treatment by checking off Yes or No by each person.

Kids younger than you?   __Yes __No

People you don't like?   __Yes __No

People in prison?   __Yes __No

People who treat you fairly?   __Yes __No

Now read this:

God does not show favoritism. (Acts 10:34)

Does knowing this change your view
of who deserves fairness?   __Yes __No

Why or why not?

_____

_____

_____

_____

_____

Loving

I should love myself first so I can love others better.

Love your neighbor as yourself.

~ Matthew 22:39

Love Yourself

Heather stood in front of the mirror brushing her hair. First she brushed it to the right, then to the left, and finally straight back.

"I give up!" she said as she threw down the brush. "Nothing helps–every day is a bad hair day for me. Guess it goes along with my big nose and bony legs."

Her twin sister, Paige, asked, "Why are you so hard on yourself?"

"Why don't you buzz off?" Heather snapped.

"Excuuuuse me!" said Paige, offended. "I just wondered since you announced to the world that you're a good candidate for the ugly award."

"I just want to look like Annie or be graceful like Sam."

"That makes you ugly–just because you don't look or act like someone you think is super-cool?" asked Paige. "I look like you. So would you call me ugly?"

Heather shrugged her shoulders.

"You know you wouldn't," said Paige. "Would you call Mrs. Bailey ugly?"

Mrs. Bailey was their piano teacher. The twins liked her and thought of her as an older sister or a young aunt.

"Of course not!" Heather exclaimed.

"So if you don't treat others that way, why treat yourself that way?" asked Paige. "You can't love others and be nice to them if you don't love yourself."

Heather was ready to shoot back a smart remark, but she couldn't think of one. Instead, she started brushing her hair again. This time she piled it on top of her head. The results made her laugh out loud. Paige joined in!

Your Turn

1. Why is it important to love yourself? How will loving yourself help you love your neighbor?

_____

_____

2. What are some ways you can show love to your neighbor? To yourself?

_____

_____

Prayer

Father, help me to love myself and others as You love me. Amen.

Love Meter

What do you love about yourself? Take a colored pencil and color in the spot on the love meter that tells how you feel about you.

The way I show I'm a Christian

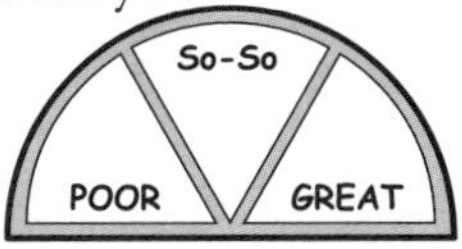

The way I look

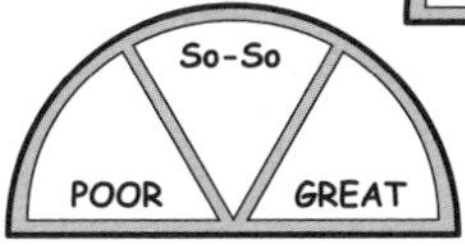

The things I can do

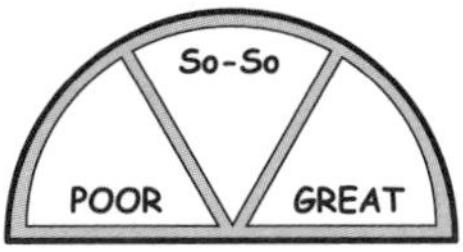

The way I think and act most of the time

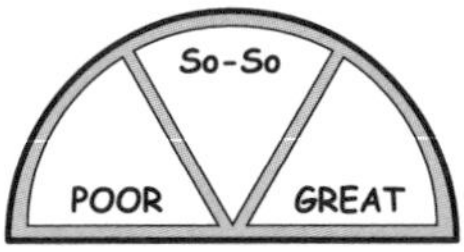

The way I treat others

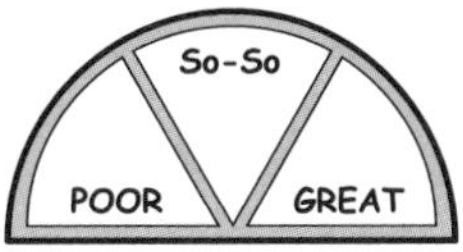

How can you improve the ones that are in the "poor" area?

_____

_____

How can you use the "great" things to help others and show love to them?

_____

_____

The Apostle Paul wrote, "Do not think of yourself more highly than you ought" (Romans 12:3). Can you ever love yourself too much? Why or why not?

_____

_____

149

Loving
I should show love to "unloved" people.

I tell you the truth, whatever you did for one of the least of these brothers of mine, you did for me.

~ Matthew 25:40

Valentine Party

"This will be the coolest party ever!" Keesha said excitedly.

"You said it, girl," Selina agreed as she high-fived her friend. "But we'd better get busy or this party will never happen!"

Both girls were sitting at a dining room table that was heaped with colored paper, lace doilies, stickers, markers, scissors and glue. They sang along with their favorite CD as they worked.

"Whoa! What's happening?" asked Selina's oldest sister, Tia, as she came into the room.

"Mom said we could have a valentine party here so we're making invitations. Then we need to decide on food, games and music," explained Selina.

"Sounds like fun," said Tia.

"Yeah, except for one thing," complained Keesha. "We have to invite all the girls in our sixth-grade homeroom. There are some we'd rather forget about."

Selina chimed in, "Becky and Andrea just don't fit in. They're so out of it in the way they dress and think. No one has much to do with them."

Tia was quiet a minute and then said, "Those girls need to be the first ones invited. They probably need your love and friendship more than anyone else. Remember that Jesus said when you are friends with someone who has no friends, you are being His friend."

Your Turn

1. Do you know someone who seems unlovable? How can you show love to him or her?

_____

_____

2. Do you think it's possible to love people you don't like? Why or why not?

_____

_____

Prayer

Lord, I don't always want to love others. Help me to love them anyway. Amen.

Perfect Heart

Hearts are fun to make and give to people you like—or to keep for yourself. They can be used to make valentines, decorations or in any way you please. But sometimes it's hard to make a heart that isn't lopsided. Here's a pattern for a perfect heart every time!

What You Need

compass

paper

scissors

ruler

pencil

cellophane tape

What to Do

1. Draw a circle on a piece of paper using the compass.

2. Cut out the circle and fold it in half.

3. Measure the folded edge of the circle.

4. Make a square with the sides the same length as the folded edge of the circle.

5. Cut out the square.

6. Cut the circle in half on the folded edge.

7. Tape half the circle on one of the square's edges and the other half on the edge next to it.

8. Use this as a pattern for making perfect hearts!

Loving

I should love the unloving.

Love one another, for love comes from God.

~ 1 John 4:7

Babysitting Blues

Sierra only had to listen to her mother's phone conversation for a few minutes to get a huge knot in her stomach. She shook her head vigorously and waved her arms in the air, but Mrs. Morris just said, "I'll ask her, Ruth. I'm sure she would be happy to watch the kids for a few hours. Bye."

When her mother hung up the phone, Sierra said, "No, no, no! I do not want to watch the Bradley kids. They are terrible. The twins are always fighting and complaining. And James thinks he's too big to have to listen to me now that he's 8."

"Mrs. Bradley has an important business luncheon on Saturday and can't find anyone to stay with the kids," Mom said. "I told her you would let her know tonight."

"Mo-o-om!" Sierra wailed. "I can see why no one wants to sit for her. Sometimes I don't think anyone in that house likes each other."

"I know they aren't very loving neighbors sometimes," said Mom. "But we don't have to act the same way. That's why God helps us love those we have a hard time loving."

Sierra almost smiled as she said, "Okay. I'll load up on loving and wear them down with kindness on Saturday."

Your Turn

1. Think of someone you have a hard time loving. How do you usually respond to that person?

_____

_____

2. What do you think God wants you to do?

_____

Prayer

Loving God, I have a hard time loving some people. Help me to love the unlovable. Amen.

Loving For the Heart and Tummy

Let your family know that they are loved. Surprise them with these loving treats.

What You Need

½" x 3" strips of paper
pencil
Bible
graham crackers
canned frosting

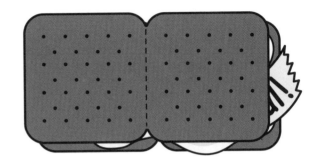

What to Do

1. Write a "loving" message on the strips of paper. (Some ideas: "God loves you;" "You are special;" "You are nice;" "You make me happy.")

2. Spread a thin layer of frosting on a graham cracker.

3. Lay on a paper strip, with a part of it sticking out to the side.

4. Add a cracker top.

5. Serve the treats at dinner. Have each person read his or her message to the others.

Growing Up

Peaceful

God helps me feel peaceful when I feel afraid.

You, Lord, give true peace. You give peace to those who depend on you. You give peace to those who trust you.

~ Isaiah 26:3 ICB

The Report (Part 1)

As Julia Tompkins walked the four blocks to school, that sinking feeling returned. She had felt it for days. Today was oral report day–the most hated of all days. She had to talk about a book that she had read. Julia felt as if she would rather wrestle an alligator than talk in class.

She passed a shaky hand through her short, dark hair. As she walked, the thought came to her to pray. "Whenever you're feeling scared, pray," her Sunday school teacher had said.

Julia shrugged. *Couldn't hurt...God, I'm scared to do this. Will You help me?*

As she neared the school, Julia suddenly noticed that the sinking feeling was gone. Instead, she felt calm. The calm lasted until she had to give her report, then she started to get nervous again. But after a quick prayer, she felt calm once more. Even though her voice shook as she talked about the book, she still felt peaceful.

Finally, it was over.

Thanks, God, she prayed.

Your Turn

1. How did Julia feel about giving the report?

_____

_____

2. How did God help her?

_____

_____

3. Think of a time when you needed to feel peaceful. What did you do? If you need peace now, use the prayer below.

_____

_____

Prayer

Lord, I need Your peace about _____ (fill in a situation that bothers you). Thank You for providing peace in my life. Amen.

156

Before and After

Many people in the Bible faced scary problems. Read the Scriptures below. Write about how you think each person felt and how God helped him or her.

Hannah

How did Hannah feel? (1 Samuel 1:10-11)

_____

How did God help? (1 Samuel 1:17)

_____

How do you think Hannah felt then? (1 Samuel 1:18)

_____

Jehoshaphat

How did Jehoshaphat feel? (2 Chronicles 20:2-3)

_____

How did God help? (2 Chronicles 20:15)

_____

How do you think Jehoshaphat felt then?
(2 Chronicles 20:18)

_____

Hezekiah

How did Hezekiah feel? (2 Kings 20:1-3, Isaiah 38:14)

_____

How did God help? (2 Kings 20:4-5)

_____

How do you think Hezekiah felt then?
(2 Kings 20:4-5, Isaiah 38:15, 20)

_____

Peaceful

Even though I have God's peace, I still will have hard times.

The Lord gives strength to his people; the Lord blesses his people with peace.

~ Psalm 29:11

The Report (Part 2)

Julia Tompkins smiled as she let herself in the apartment that afternoon after school. She grabbed a package of cheese and crackers, then sat in the living room and smiled at her grandfather. As usual, he was in his favorite spot: the recliner.

"How did your book report go?" Grandpa asked. "I see that you survived. You didn't think you would."

Julia's smile widened. "It went okay."

Grandpa grinned in response. "You seem pretty calm. I know you were nervous about doing it."

"I prayed as I walked to school. I felt peaceful." Julia shrugged. "I would've felt more peaceful if I didn't have to do it at all."

Her grandfather leaned over and chucked her under the chin. "Being peaceful doesn't mean avoiding what you have to do. God gives you peace and strength to do what you have to do."

Your Turn

1. Turn back to page 156. How was Julia's mood as she walked to school different from how she was after school?

_____

_____

2. Do you think having peace means not going through hard times? Why or why not?

_____

_____

3. Do you or someone you know need peace? Turn the Scripture above into prayer like the one below.

_____

_____

Prayer

Lord, You promise in the Bible to give strength to your people and to bless us with peace. I'm counting on You for that. Amen.

Peace like a River

Read the words of the song "Peace like a River" below. This song is based on Philippians 4:7. Say the words to yourself. If you know the words, sing it. Is this song true about you?

I've got peace like a river,

I've got peace like a river,

I've got peace like a river in my soul;

I've got peace like a river,

I've got peace like a river,

I've got peace like a river in my soul.

Peaceful

God wants me to seek peaceful solutions to problems.

Turn from evil and do good; seek peace and pursue it.

~ Psalm 34:14

Rancorous Roni

"Hey, Roni, what's the opposite of 'rancorous'?"

Veronica Nesbitt fell totally silent when her older brother, Tom, asked that question. She had just thought up a mental list of people who had made her mad at school. If only she could get even with Bailey for what she said during lunch.

"Why are you asking me that stupid question?" Veronica asked after a few moments of silence. "I don't even know what 'rancorous' means."

Tom looked up from his homework and grinned. "I do. It means bitter or hostile. That sounds like you all right."

Veronica slammed her math book shut, wishing she had studied in her room instead of joining her brother at the kitchen table. "You just made my list!"

"What list? Your I'm mad-at-so-and-so list?" Tom made a face. "You're always mad at somebody these days. That's all you ever say: 'I'm so mad!'" He did a pretty fair imitation, which made Veronica laugh, despite how mad he made her.

"Instead of always getting mad at somebody, why don't you do something that will keep a friend instead of losing one?" Tom asked.

"Why don't you mind your own business?" Veronica tossed back at him.

Your Turn

1. Why was Veronica angry?

_____

_____

2. What was Tom's advice?

_____

_____

3. What advice would you have for Veronica, based on the verse above?

_____

_____

Prayer

Lord, help me to pursue peaceful relationships with my family and friends, and to not hold grudges. Please help me to be an example of peace to others. Amen.

A Peaceful Scene

There are seven things wrong with this "peaceful" scene. See if you can spot them all. One of the seven can be changed to make the scene more peaceful. What could be done?

The solution is on page 236.

Courageous

God gives me the courage to face tough situations.

Have I not commanded you? Be strong and courageous. Do not be terrified; do not be discouraged, for the Lord your God is with you wherever you go.

~ Joshua 1:9

First Day of School

New neighborhood. New school. In the summer, Santina Esqueda had been excited about the move to Carroll Park. But now that the first day of school was two days away, fear was setting in.

As she stared at her reflection in the mirror, Santina couldn't help worrying about the first day of sixth grade. *What if everyone hates me at this school? What if I don't make any friends?*

"You were awfully quiet at dinner tonight, *niña* [little one]," her mother suddenly said from the doorway.

"What if everyone hates me at this school?" Santina blurted out. She turned a worried face to her mother.

"Is that what's been bothering you?" Mrs. Esqueda moved farther into the room. "Don't forget you can ask God to give you the courage to face whatever you have to face."

Santina nodded. She hadn't prayed. In fact, she hadn't thought about God at all. The thought of God suddenly made her feel better.

Your Turn

1. Why was Santina afraid?

_____

_____

2. What was her mother's advice?

_____

_____

3. When are you most afraid? Memorize Joshua 1:9. When you're afraid, remember this promise from God.

_____

_____

Prayer

Thank You, Lord, for the courage You give. Amen.

The Courage to Trust

Courage comes from trusting God. Psalm 28:7 has good advice about doing that. To figure out the advice, put the letters below each column in the boxes above that column. The letters may not be listed in the exact order in which they appear in the quote. Mark off used letters at the bottom. A letter may only be used once. The black boxes stand for the end of a word.

```
G A N D R T D A M E  S E H P I D D R M Y
T H E A A O T D M Y  H S L Y E N T H E M
  H H   L N R   R I  S T S I E S       I N
  T E       I        M       L
```

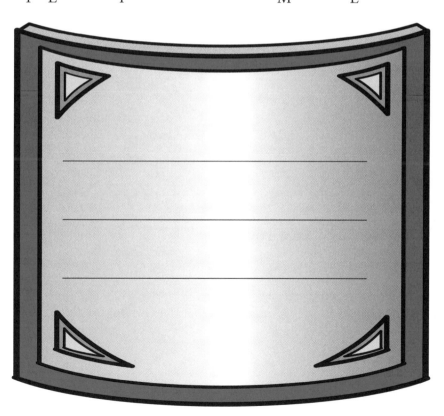

The solution is on page 236.

Courageous

Being courageous sometimes means saying no to wrong behavior.

Be on your guard; stand firm in the faith; be men of courage; be strong.

~ 1 Corinthians 16:13

Just Say No?

Allison Tobias waited while Jenna Ervin ran to catch up with her in the school hallway.

"So, you coming to my sleepover?" Jenna asked as the girls walked toward the school bus. "We're gonna tell ghost stories and call the psychic hotline. My mom has given us permission to do it. My older sister's going to call for us. Won't that be fun?"

Allison nodded, even though she didn't think the last idea sounded like fun. Last Sunday, the youth pastor at her church had talked against using psychic hotlines. "It's playing with the occult," he had said.

Allison sighed. She badly wanted to be Jenna's friend. Most of the girls in the fifth grade did. Jenna's family lived in a large house with two horses in a stable out back. Allison loved horses. Being invited to a sleepover was a dream come true. Yet she knew that Jenna wasn't a Christian.

I know Mom wouldn't want me to go if she knew what we'd be doing, she thought. *I've got to tell Jenna I can't do it. But what if she laughs at me?*

Your Turn

1. Read the Scripture above. What advice would you give Allison? Why?

_____

_____

_____

2. What would you do if you were Allison? Why?

_____

_____

3. Have you ever been in this situation? What did you do?

_____

_____

Prayer

Lord, give me the courage to stand up for what I believe. Amen.

A Message for You

Need a pep talk about courage? Thought so! Cross out the Bs, Cs, Ks, and Ms to find a message about courage.

The solution is on page 236.

G ⟍⟍O⟍⟍DWIN⟍⟍⟍LL⟍HE⟍⟍L⟍P
⟍Y⟍⟍OU.
J⟍U⟍S⟍T⟍⟍⟍⟍V⟍EFA⟍⟍I⟍TH⟍⟍!

_____

_____

_____

Courageous

God's presence gives me the courage to go anywhere.

"Never will I leave you; never will I forsake you." So we say with confidence,
"The Lord is my helper; I will not be afraid. What can man do to me?"

~ Hebrews 13:5-6

The Blank Key

Leanne Reynolds pointed toward the TV. "I wouldn't go in that room without the Blank Key," she said. A door leading to a dark room suddenly appeared on the screen. "You'll get clobbered instantly by the fear creatures. The Blank Key is a weapon and opens any door in the game."

Her friend, Abby, who had the game system controls, nodded. "Whew! Thanks for telling me, Le."

"Why are you two hogging the TV?" Abby's older brother, Jason, asked. He stood in the doorway to the family room. Both girls jumped.

Abby tossed a sofa pillow at him. "Go away!"

She turned back to Leanne, as if Jason hadn't spoken. "This key is awesome. I wish I had something like this in real life. I wouldn't be afraid of anything!"

Jason flopped on the couch behind where the girls sat on the floor. "You've got something better than some old key! God goes with you everywhere you go, right? Because of Him, you don't have to fear anything."

Leanne and Abby exchanged a look.

"Anyway, I've played this game before. That key won't work against the slithering monsters on the next level."

Leanne and Abby groaned.

"Good thing God can do anything, huh?"

"Be quiet, Jason," Abby said.

Your Turn

1. According to Jason, what is the real "key" to courage?

_____

_____

2. Do you believe him? Why or why not?

_____

_____

Prayer

God, I'm thankful that You are always with me. Knowing that helps me to be courageous! Amen.

A Promise to Keep

Want to memorize Hebrews 13:5-6? You can begin right now. First, go back to page 166 and reread the Scripture. Then come back to this page. See if you can say the verse by filling in the missing words. (No peeking at page 166, unless you absolutely must!) Say the verse several times to yourself. The solution is on page 236.

"Never _____ I _____ you; _____ will I _____

you." So we say with _____, "The Lord is my _____; I will

not be _____. What can man do to _____?"

~ Hebrews 13:5-6

Confident

I should have the confidence to say no.

For the Lord will be your confidence and will keep your foot from being snared.

~ Proverbs 3:26

Joining the Group

"I thought you wanted to be part of our group. Are you a 'fraidy cat?"

Jaylene stood in front of the convenience store, hands on her hips. She was staring at Donya, waiting for an answer. The other girls were looking at her, too.

Donya thought about Jaylene's one rule for becoming part of the group: Each girl had to shoplift some small thing from the store without getting caught.

Donya knew that was wrong, but Jaylene and her friends were the coolest kids in sixth grade. Donya was flattered when Jaylene asked if she wanted to be part of their group. She thought that would be really neat. But now she was changing her mind.

Lord, give me the confidence to say no, Donya prayed silently.

Jaylene gave her a little push toward the store. "I can't do it," Donya said quietly.

"Chicky, chicky," one girl teased. "You're scared."

Donya nodded. "Guess I am scared. But more than that, shoplifting is stealing, and stealing is wrong."

Donya left the group and went on home. On the way she silently said, *Thanks for giving me the confidence, God, to turn them down.*

Your Turn

1. Is your confidence in God strong enough to see you through troubles? Why or why not?

_____

_____

2. If not, how can you raise your confidence in Him?

_____

_____

Prayer

Lord, give me confidence to always rely on You and trust You to do what's best. Amen.

Loads of Confidence

Many Bible people had loads of confidence in God. They were confident He would be with them and help them no matter what. Fit their names into the grid below.

Abednego
Abraham
Daniel
David
Elijah
Esther
James
John

Joseph
Mary
Meshach
Moses
Noah
Paul
Peter
Shadrach
Silas

The solution is on page 237.

Confident

People may not always live up to the confidence I have in them.

It is better to trust the Lord than to put confidence in people.

~ Psalm 118:8 NLT

Science Project

"I don't believe it! What a traitor! I can't believe she did that!" Valerie stomped around the kitchen punctuating her words by shaking her fists.

"Did somebody sell your secret diary to the newspaper?" her brother Joe asked.

Valerie gave him an angry stare. "Don't be such a jerk!"

"All right. Cool it," their mother ordered. "Now, Valerie, what are you so hot and bothered about?"

"The science fair is in two days. There are four kids in our group and each of us picked which part of the project to do. Tomorrow we're meeting at Russell's house and putting all the parts together. Russell called and said Sandra told him she was too busy and she didn't have anything done. For two weeks she said she was working on it and knew just what to do–she didn't need any help. She seemed so confident and sure of herself. We trusted her and believed she'd do what she said. Now she ditches us and the three of us have to scramble around and fill in."

"I'm sorry Sandra didn't live up to the confidence you had in her," her mother said. "Why don't you call Russell and Tiffany and have them come here after supper? Maybe I can help you fill in the missing pieces."

"Thanks, Mom. Hope you remember your science teaching days," said Valerie as she hurried to the phone.

Your Turn

1. What happens when you lose confidence in someone? How do you feel?

_____

_____

2. How does it help you to know that you can always put your confidence in God?

_____

_____

Prayer

Lord, I am confident that You will always do what You promise. Help me to follow Your example. Amen.

Trust In God

You can always put your confidence in God and trust Him completely. A Scripture about trust is hidden in this puzzle. To find the Scripture, skip every other letter in two trips around the circle. Print the letters on the blanks inside the circle.

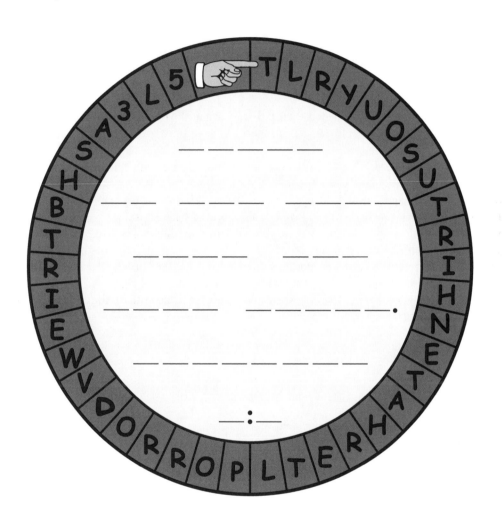

The solution is on page 237.

Confident

I should be confident of my God-given abilities.

*Such confidence as this is ours through Christ before
God...our competence comes from God.*

~ 2 Corinthians 3:4-5

Good Enough?

Teela was picking at her dinner, taking a few bites and pushing the rest around the plate. Her food-pushing was accompanied by a lot of sighing.

"What's with all the dramatics? You sound like a sick cow," complained her older brother, Mike.

"Enough already," warned their father. Teela and Mike were known to get into some pretty heated arguments. "But you do seem to have something on your mind, Teela," he added.

Teela nodded. "Coach Woods wants me to be the starting forward in tomorrow's basketball game against Hillcrest. They're a tough team and I don't know if I'm good enough to start against them. What if I really goof up?"

Her father reached over to give her a pat on the back. "God gave you quickness and strength. He also gave you a good brain. You know how to play. Just be confident and believe you can do it."

"I'll remember how I sometimes outscore my big bad brother when we shoot hoops in the driveway," Teela said with a teasing grin.

"You asked for it, kid," responded Mike. "Meet you in the driveway in 15 minutes!"

Your Turn

1. Have you ever felt like Teela? What did you do?

_____

_____

2. What gives you confidence in your ability to do something?

_____

Prayer

God, I know I can always be confident of Your love and care. Thanks. Amen.

Godly Confidence

To find a Bible verse about true confidence, follow these directions.

The solution is on page 237.

Cross out the last letter of each line.

Cross out all the numbers except 1 and 7.

Cross out the Cs and Zs in line 2.

Cross out animal names in lines 1 and 8.

Cross out the Bs and Gs in line 3.

Cross out colors in lines 4 and 6.

Cross out girls' names in line 5.

Cross out boys' names in line 7.

Circle the leftover letters and write the words they make on the lines below.

1) C A T B L 6 E S S E D C O W Y

2) 8 I Z S T 3 H E Z M 9 A C N P

3) W B 4 H O G T 5 R U B S T S G

4) I N G O L D T H E B L A C K S

5) P E G L O R D L U W H O S E R

6) P I N K C O N F I D E N C E L

7) J O E I S I N P A U L H I M W

8) D O G J E R . 1 8 7 7 F I S H S

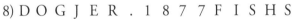

173

Self-disciplined

Self-discipline means being motivated to change my behavior.

Be patient and stand firm.

~ James 5:8

All at Once or Wait?

Sarah Augenstein quickly pointed her friend Nia in the opposite direction from the one Mrs. Augenstein took. She barely heard her mother say, "Sarah, I want you girls to meet me at this entrance in an hour. Then we'll go the movie theater."

"I can't wait to spend my allowance!" Sarah cried. The money seemed to burn a hole in her purse.

"Not me. I'm saving my money," said Nia.

"I can't save money. Spending it is too much fun. My dad says I'm a spend-o-holic." Sarah looked proud of her father's description.

"I used to be, too, but I started telling myself, 'Just wait. You don't have to spend everything all at once.'"

Sarah paused by a pretzel shop. "Wanna get a pretzel?"

Nia shook her head. "Aren't we going to stop at McDonald's after the movie? I'll wait 'til then."

Sarah stared at Nia. "Are you for real?"

Nia smiled. "I'm just trying to be patient. I like to wait until I get exactly what I want." She paused. "Whenever I want to spend, I just tell myself, 'No. Just wait.' So I do."

Sarah shook her head. She couldn't imagine going without what she wanted when she wanted it.

Your Turn

1. Being self-disciplined means motivating yourself to do something really hard. It also means correcting your behavior if necessary. What was Nia self-disciplined about?

_____

_____

2. Being self-disciplined involves patience and self-control. When it comes to both, would you say you're more like Sarah or like Nia? Why?

_____

_____

Prayer

Lord, I want to learn to be more self-disciplined. Please show me how. Amen.

Ready For Anything?

Use the acrostic below to list some things you need to motivate yourself to do or some behaviors you need to correct in order to be more self-disciplined. Use words that begin with each letter. For example, you might need to be self-disciplined about Scripture memorization (S). Or maybe you need to be self-disciplined about EVERYTHING (E)!

S_____

E_____

L_____

F_____

D_____

I_____

S_____

C_____

I_____

P_____

L_____

I_____

N_____

E_____

D_____

Self-disciplined

Being self-disciplined means being prepared.

For God did not give us a spirit of timidity, but a spirit of power, of love and of self-discipline.

~ 2 Timothy 1:7

Fear of Failure

Laura Webb took one look at her social studies textbook, then dropped her head in the middle of it. "I'm gonna fail next week's test! I just know it!" she wailed.

Iris Klausmeier, who was in her fifth-grade study group, poked her with the eraser end of a pencil. "You've got a whole week to study! So what're you whining about?"

Laura raised her head, but her face was hidden behind a curtain of light brown hair. "But I haven't been studying." She paused. "You sound calm. I'll bet you're already prepared for the test."

Iris looked smug. "I've been studying for it for two weeks."

Laura threw her friend a look. "I don't see how you do it. You never seem afraid that you'll fail."

"That's because I try to be prepared. But I wasn't always like that. My dad taught me. Besides, I know God doesn't want us to waste time worrying over what might not happen."

Laura waited until her friend's back was turned before she silently mimicked her. Still, she knew that Iris was right.

Your Turn

1. How could she learn from Iris's example?

_____

_____

2. If you had a friend like Laura, what would you tell her based on the advice from 2 Timothy 1:7?

_____

_____

Prayer

Lord, help me not to fear, but to try my best. Amen.

Get Ready, Get Set...

Athletes work hard to discipline themselves in order to reach their goal. Christians are to be disciplined, too. Think about the questions below. What do you need to do to...

_____

_____

_____

_____

_____

_____

_____

_____

_____

Turn the page upside down to find something you can do right now.

Ask God for help to just do it!

Self-disciplined

God wants me to watch my words.

Let us be self-controlled, putting on faith and love as a breastplate, and the hope of salvation as a helmet.

~ 1 Thessalonians 5:8

A Self-disciplined Mouth

Karen Farmer shook her head as she watched her aunt say good-bye to the last customer to enter the small bookstore. She was surprised to hear her aunt's pleasant, "Thanks! Come again!"

"That was the rudest man I've ever seen!" Karen declared as soon as the door closed. "You were really nice to him, Aunt Becky." She paused. "You're always smiling and stuff. I never see you yell at anybody or even get really mad. Do you ever, like, lose it?"

Aunt Becky laughed. "I get mad at people. I yell sometimes. Your Uncle James will tell you that I used to have a really bad temper. But God helps me do better. People like that man who just left used to really set me off. Nowadays, I have to bite my tongue sometimes–literally–just to keep from saying something mean back!"

Karen laughed. "I wish I could be like you."

"Don't wish that!" said Aunt Becky. "You can ask for God's help to do whatever it takes to be like Jesus."

Your Turn

1. Watching what you say is another way to be self-disciplined. Are you ever tempted to say something unkind? What do you do during those moments?

_____

_____

2. First Thessalonians 5:8 is a reminder to put on faith and love. That means to remember you belong to God. How can knowing that you belong to God help you when you're tempted to say something unkind to someone else?

_____

_____

Prayer

God, help me to behave in such a way that everyone will know that I'm Your child. Amen.

Your Award Reward

Have you made progress in being self-disciplined? If so, give yourself an award. For what do you deserve an award? Did you stop procrastinating (putting things off)? Did you memorize Scripture? Did you break a bad habit? Finish coloring an award below.

Joyfulness

I can be joyful no matter what my circumstances are.

Be joyful in hope, patient in affliction, faithful in prayer.

~ Romans 12:12

The Visit

Grace Phelps wasn't sure what she had expected when she went to visit her cousins. But smiles and laughter were not what she had anticipated. After all, her uncle still had not found a job. Yet her three cousins and her uncle and aunt greeted her at the door with hugs and plenty of laughter.

During a break in the action, Grace followed her aunt to the kitchen. "Do you guys have good news?" she asked her Aunt Phyllis. "Did Uncle Simon find a job?"

"No, not yet," Aunt Phyllis replied.

"Oh, but I thought…" Grace didn't want to say what she thought.

"You thought you'd find us sitting around with long faces?" Her aunt laughed. "God has helped us so far. We've been able to pay our bills. I can't say it's been easy, but God is still good. The joy He gives is something no one can take away."

Grace stared at her, amazed. "Wow! I thought I came to cheer you up. You've cheered me up instead!"

Your Turn

1. What did Grace expect to find at her uncle and aunt's house?

_____

_____

2. Joy isn't the same as happiness. A person is usually happy when everything goes right in her life. Joy, however, is a gift of God. Knowing what God has done for you should give you joy. Which would you rather have: joy or
   happiness? Why?

_____

_____

Prayer

I praise You, Lord, for the joy You provide. Amen.

Today's Verse

Solve the puzzle by substituting the letters for the numbers.

KEY

A	B	C	D	E	F	G	H	I	J
2	9	14	22	11	23	8	1	16	12

K	L	M	N	O	P	Q	R	S	T
4	13	7	3	17	21	6	24	10	15

U	V	W	X	Y	Z
18	26	19	25	20	5

9 11   12 17 20 23 18 13   16 3   1 17 21 11

___   _____   ___   _____

21 2 15 16 11 3 15   16 3   2 23 23 13 16 14 15 16 17 3

_____   ___   _____

23 2 16 15 1 23 18 13   16 3

_____   ___

21 24 2 20 11 24.   24 17 7 2 3 10

_____   _____ 12:12

The solution is on page 237.

Joyfulness

God wants me to always be joyful.

Rejoice in the Lord always. I will say it again: Rejoice!

~ Philippians 4:4

Elizabeth's Praise

"As we close in prayer, all who wish to can share a sentence of praise."

Rachel Edmonton closed her eyes, but she was not one of the ones who "wished to share a sentence of praise."

What do I have to be thankful about? she thought. Rachel's parents had cancelled the family's planned trip to the beach that summer. "Money is tight this year," her mother had said.

At first there was silence. Rachel opened one eye and gave the other kids in her Sunday school class a quick glance. She noticed other eyes open as well.

Suddenly, a soft voice began. "God, thanks for always being with us."

Rachel was surprised to hear Elizabeth speak. If anyone had a right to be miserable, it was Elizabeth. Her father had been sick off and on that year. Her mother had died two years ago.

When the prayer ended, Rachel was doubly surprised at the smile on Elizabeth's face. But then, Elizabeth was always smiling.

What's with her? Rachel thought.

She suddenly thought of the memory verse they had discussed: "Rejoice in the Lord always."

Hmmph, Rachel thought. *I don't feel like rejoicing.*

Your Turn

1. Should you wait until you feel like rejoicing? Why or why not?

_____

_____

2. When hard times come, do you usually respond like Rachel or like Elizabeth? (Be honest!)

_____

_____

Prayer

God, I rejoice in knowing You. Amen.

Clues to Cross-Out

Use the following clues to know which words to cross out in the chart below. The leftover words provide good advice when hard times come. To read the advice, start in the left column and read the words up and down all the way to the right.

Cross Out

1. the seasons of the year
2. girl names
3. words that are numbers
4. names of Bible people

The solution is on page 237.

Barbara	of	three	Abraham
seven	Spring	Nadia	thoughts,
Instead	Peter	sad	Summer
Winter	thinking	Fall	rejoice

Joyfulness

I can express my joy to God.

Shout with joy to God, all the earth!

~ Psalm 66:1

Give a Shout!

As soon as Cinnamon Philip's last whoop died, she noticed her mother standing in the doorway leading down to the basement. She gave her mother a wide smile, showing pink braces.

"What on earth is all that racket down here?" Mrs. Philip asked. "I heard you clear outside."

Cinnamon pointed to the TV. "They won! My favorite soccer team won the championship! Yeeeeeeessss!" She ran to the stairs to give her mother a high-five.

Mrs. Philip smiled. "Never let it be said that my daughter has no lungs."

"Oh, Mommmm! I can't help it if I'm happy." Cinnamon gave another shout of joy.

Mrs. Philip folded her arms. "Hmm. You tell me all the time that you're happy about being a Christian. I don't hear you make this much noise in church."

"Moooooommmm!" Cinnamon groaned. After a second's pause, she suddenly yelled, "Yea, God!"

Then she grinned at her mother. "There!"

Your Turn

1. What was Cinnamon happy about?

_____

_____

2. What are you usually the most "vocal" about?

_____

_____

3. Why is it important to "shout with joy to God, all the earth" as Psalm 66:1 suggests?

_____

_____

Prayer

Oh, God, may Your name be praised. Amen.

 **Yea, God!**

Share your joy in the Lord by filling in the speech balloon. You can make up a cheer for God or use pictures.

Teachable

I should believe the true things I have been taught.

Continue in what you have learned and have become convinced of,
because you know those from whom you learned it.

~ 2 Timothy 3:14

Different Ideas

All night the wind whistled around the house and sleet pinged against the windows. Megan snuggled down under the covers, but she had a hard time sleeping. It wasn't just the icy storm that was keeping her awake. She kept thinking about some things that had happened in school that day.

The next morning, everything was covered with ice—it looked like a fairyland.

"No school today," Megan's mom announced at breakfast. "It's too dangerous for the buses to be out. What are you going to do with your free day?"

Megan just shrugged her shoulders and stared at her oatmeal.

"What's bothering you, Megs?" her dad asked. "Would you rather go to school?"

"School is very confusing right now," Megan said. "I'm hearing all different kinds of ideas and I have trouble sorting them out. In biology, the teacher talks about evolution and how people evolved from other creatures over millions of years. And lots of the kids in the class think that's true, or they just don't care."

Mr. Howard patted her on the shoulder. "I know that you're very smart and learn easily. But not everything you are going to be taught is true. Remember what you have learned in church, Sunday school and Bible study. Trust the people who taught you those things and know that is what's true."

Your Turn

1. Have you ever been taught something different from what you believe to be true? What did you do?

_____

_____

2. To whom would you go if you were confused about ideas you were taught?

_____

_____

Prayer

Jesus, You are the master teacher. Help me always to be teachable when it comes to learning what You want me to know. Amen.

God, the Teacher

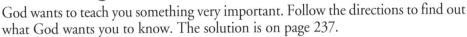

God wants to teach you something very important. Follow the directions to find out what God wants you to know. The solution is on page 237.

Color all the squares that have a * or + in them.

Color every square in which you find one of these letters: F L W.

Color each square that has an X or Z.

Color each empty square.

Read the words left in the uncolored spaces.

A		*		L	X		+		W		F
I	+			*		X		W		T	Z
+		*	F		I	*		S		L	W
	*	Z		B		X		+	Y		X
	G	+		W	R	L	A		C	*	E
	W		+		Y	F	O		*	U	Z
H	*	L		A		+	V	Z	E	L	+
+		B	*		E		F	+	E	N	W
S	*		L		A	Z	V	+	E		D
+		*		F		L		W	Z	+	X

Teachable

I should be a "teachable" learner.

I will instruct you and teach you in the way you should go.

~ Psalm 32:8

Teachable Tess

The Kolb family always talked about what they learned in Sunday school at Sunday lunch. Questions were encouraged, and some lively discussions took place.

"By the way," Mrs. Kolb said, "your Sunday school teacher talked to me about you this morning, Tess."

"Ha!" snickered Jimmy. "Probably said you flirt with all the guys!"

His twin brother, Jared, said, "No, I think she talks too much. Yackety, yackety, yackety!"

Mr. Kolb stopped all further opinions when he shot the boys one of his "you'd better cool it" looks. "Now maybe you can talk in peace," he said to his wife.

Tess had no idea what the teacher said. She sort of wished everyone would forget the conversation, but she was curious.

"Mr. Wilkens said that he really likes having you in his class, Tess," her mom continued. "He told me that you listen to the lesson and ask questions about what you don't understand. Sometimes your questions make the other kids ask their own questions. All of this leads to searching for answers in the Bible. Mr. Wilkens said you were very teachable."

"'Teachable Tess,'" her dad said. "That has a nice ring to it."

Jimmy and Jared looked at each other and rolled their eyes. "And what would your Sunday school teacher say about you guys?" their dad asked.

Neither one answered as they dug into their desserts.

Your Turn

1. Why is it important to be teachable? Why would this be especially important when you are studying the Bible?

_____

_____

2. Are you teachable? If not, how can you improve?

_____

_____

Prayer

Lord, I have many things to learn. Help me to be teachable. Amen.

Things I'd Like to Know

Do you know how to swim, play a musical instrument, cook or play a great game of checkers? You probably know how to do lots of things. But what are some things you don't know how to do and would like to learn? Try to think of one or two things to go with each of the letters below.

T
E _____
A _____
C _____
H _____

M _____
E _____

189

Attentive

God wants me to pay attention to His Word.

We must pay more careful attention, therefore, to what we have heard, so that we do not drift away.

~ Hebrews 2:1

Atten-hut!

As usual, the youth church noise had reached a high pitch. Jeff Wallace, one of the youth pastors, waved two fingers in the air. That was the sign for quiet.

"Atten-hut!" He usually said that when he wanted attention. "Our topic today is on that very subject: paying attention. That means you, Eva."

Eva Miller suddenly stopped whispering to her friend Natalie. They both grinned.

"God wants us to pay attention to what He has said in the Bible. He wants us to listen with our ears as well as our hearts. Why do you suppose that's important? Eva, what do you think?"

Once more, Eva had been caught talking to her friend. "Because we're supposed to?"

"Yes, but paying attention also helps us to stick close to God."

After the meeting, Eva went up to the youth pastor. "I'm sorry I wasn't paying attention."

Pastor Jeff smiled. "Well, at least you knew to come up to confess. You must have been paying some attention."

Your Turn

1. Was Eva paying attention? Why or why not?

_____

_____

2. How do you think paying attention to what God says in the Bible can help

you to avoid "drifting away" as Hebrews 2:1 says?

_____

_____

Prayer

Open my eyes and ears, Lord, to Your truth. Amen.

Your Attention, Please!

Pay attention to the scene below for the next three minutes. Then use a piece of paper to cover up the picture. (No peeking!) Turn this page upside down. Answer the questions to see how much you remember about the picture. Were you paying attention?

4. Was the jump rope on the bed or near it?

3. Name at least two other items on her desk.

2. What stuffed animal sat on her desk?

1. What was the girl reading?

191

Attentive

God wants me to be wise about the messages to which I pay attention.

Do not pay attention to every word people say.

~ Ecclesiastes 7:21

The Rumor

Tonesha Davis clicked on the icon labeled "Kids Only" chat room. Some of her friends planned to log on at 6:30. She glanced at the clock: 6:27.

They'll be on soon, she thought. *Might as well log on myself.*

Tonesha joined a discussion about her favorite author.

She typed: `I've read all of Casey Martin's books. I can't wait for her new one to come out.`

Someone with the screen name "EekCat" replied: `She's not really a Christian.`

Tonesha: `How do you know?`

EekCat: `Someone in another chat room told me that. In fact, I heard she was once in prison.`

Tonesha's heart gave a sick lurch. *That can't be true…can it?* she asked herself.

Suddenly Tonesha's friend Renee entered the discussion. Her screen name was Ren123.

`That is totally bogus. There was a notice up in the chat room about that rumor. It's totally false. You shouldn't spread lies like that.`

EekCat suddenly dropped out of the conversation.

Tonesha's parents had warned her about not believing everything she read. "Some people don't tell the truth," her father had said.

That is the truth, Tonesha thought as she called Renee about what she was going to wear to Sydney's birthday party.

Your Turn

1. What did EekCat want Tonesha to believe?

_____

_____

2. Why do you think her parents told her not to believe everything she read?

_____

_____

Prayer

Lord, show me what to pay attention to and what to avoid. Amen.

God's Way of Getting Attention

God sometimes uses unusual ways to get our attention. An Old Testament king named Belshazzar did not believe in God. But he received the shock of his life one day! Connect the dots to find what Belshazzar saw. Then hold up this page to a mirror to find out what God did. Both answers complete the sentence. You can find this story in Daniel 5. The solution is on page 237.

Belshazzar saw a _____.

God used to _____.

WRITE ON THE WALL

Attentive

I can grow in wisdom by paying attention to my parents' advice.

Listen…to a father's instruction; pay attention and gain understanding.

~ Proverbs 4:1

Are You Listening?

"Cy-bill, are you listening to me?"

Cybill Reid half-heard her three-year-old brother, Tyler, talking. He talked nonstop sometimes. Most of her attention was reserved for the program blasting from the TV. Then suddenly, the TV went black.

"Mom! Cable's out!" Cybill yelled.

Her mother stuck her head in the family room. "Not really. I turned it off."

"Moooom! I was watching something!"

"But you weren't paying attention to your brother."

"Moooom!"

"Don't 'Moooom' me. You were the one who told me you wanted to be less selfish. You said you made a decision in church to pay more attention to the needs of others."

Cybill recalled those words. She almost regretted having said anything to her mother.

"Oh, okay! What do you want, boy?" Cybill suddenly realized that Tyler had left the room.

"Where's Tyler?"

"In his room," Mrs. Reid replied.

Cybill sighed as she got up from the sofa. She felt a little sorry that she had tuned out Tyler.

Your Turn

1. How do you think her brother felt?

_____

_____

2. Is there someone you're tuning out? What could you do?

_____

_____

Prayer

Jesus, I want to pay attention to the people I love. Help me to make time to do that. Amen.

Three Important Words

Want to know how to pay attention? Two words tell you how. The third tells what happens when you follow the advice. You have to really pay attention to guess the words below! Color the shapes to see them better.

The solution is on page 238.

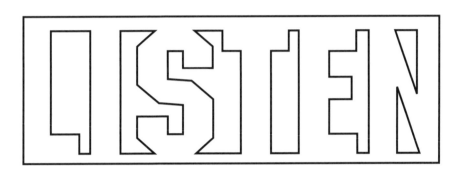

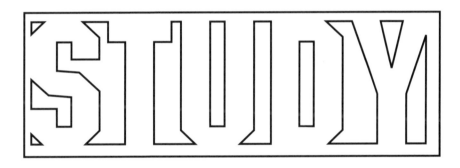

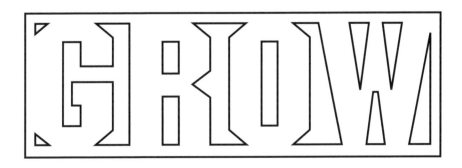

Wisdom

A wise person asks for advice.

Wisdom is found in those who take advice.

~ Proverbs 13:10

The Haircut

Maria sneaked in the side door and tiptoed to her bedroom. After she closed the door behind her, she turned to face the mirror.

She hardly recognized herself! *Why did I do this?* she wondered as she tugged at her very short black hair. *I look like I'm wearing a fuzzy black cap.*

All of the girls in Maria's sixth-grade class—at least all the popular ones—had stylish, short hairstyles. Maria wanted to look cool, too, not like a little kid with her hair hanging to her shoulders.

"Hey, Maria! Nice buzz!" hooted José when she came to dinner. Self-consciously, Maria touched her head and glared at her brother. Mr. Cortez rolled his eyes and kept quiet.

Maria's mom had a shocked look on her face. "What happened to your beautiful hair?" she asked.

"I wanted to look cool like the other girls. So I took my birthday money and got a haircut. But I don't look cool at all—I look ugly," she wailed.

"Well, you certainly look different," Mrs. Cortez said. "You are a very smart girl, but you didn't make a very wise decision. A wise person asks for advice. I'm disappointed you didn't talk to me first. Now you will have to live with your decision. Fortunately, hair grows back."

Your Turn

1. Have you ever made a decision you regretted later? What happened?

_____

_____

2. Why is it wise to ask for advice before making an important decision?

_____

_____

Prayer

God, I need wisdom to _____. Please help me. Amen.

Mathematical Wisdom

To read the secret Bible verse, do the math problems and fill in the letter found by each answer. The first letter has been done to get you started.

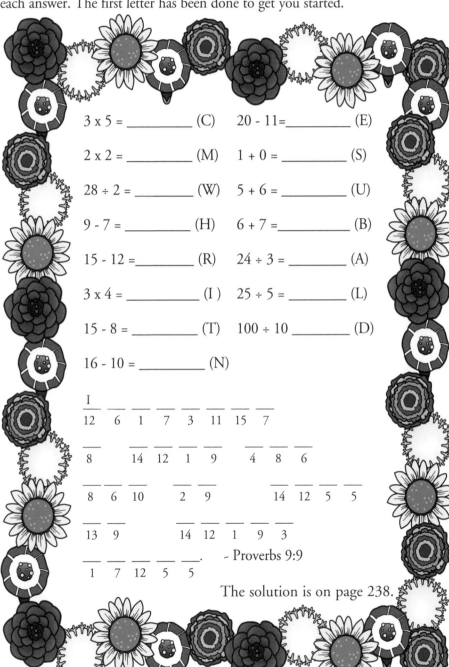

3 x 5 = _____ (C)   20 - 11=_____ (E)

2 x 2 = _____ (M)   1 + 0 = _____ (S)

28 ÷ 2 = _____ (W)   5 + 6 = _____ (U)

9 - 7 = _____ (H)   6 + 7 = _____ (B)

15 - 12 = _____ (R)   24 ÷ 3 = _____ (A)

3 x 4 = _____ (I)   25 ÷ 5 = _____ (L)

15 - 8 = _____ (T)   100 ÷ 10 _____ (D)

16 - 10 = _____ (N)

$\underset{12}{\text{I}}$ __ __ __ __ __ __ __
12 6 1 7 3 11 15 7

__ __ __ __ __ __ __ __
8   14 12 1 9   4 8 6

__ __ __ __ __ __ __ __ __
8 6 10   2 9   14 12 5 5

__ __ __ __ __ __
13 9   14 12 1 9 3

__ __ __ __ __.
1 7 12 5 5

~ Proverbs 9:9

The solution is on page 238.

Wisdom

God's Word can help me to be wise.

From infancy you have known the holy Scriptures, which are able to make you wise for salvation through faith in Christ Jesus.

~ 2 Timothy 3:15

Crazy Quilt

Great-aunt Gertrude ("Auntie" to her family) was staying with Lily's family for the winter. Auntie had arthritic knees and couldn't walk without a cane. But she always had a cheery smile and she liked being busy. Lily's father set up a quilting frame in front of a sunny window so Auntie could be in the middle of everything while she quilted.

Lily liked to watch her sew the colorful pieces together with tiny, even stitches. She also liked listening to Auntie's stories about growing up in Germany.

Each day, the quilt was a little larger and more colorful, but Lily couldn't see any kind of pattern to it.

"What do you call this quilt?" asked Lily.

Auntie laughed. "This is called a crazy quilt," she said. "The pieces are all different shapes and sizes. I just use leftover scraps of cloth and fit them together. I never know how it's going to turn out until I'm all finished.

"This quilt makes me think of my life sometimes. I'm 85 and I've had lots of different experiences–some sad and some happy. But they all fit together because of some advice I learned a long time ago when I was your age."

Lily asked, "What was that?"

"God's Word can help me be wise. It tells me that God loves me and is always with me through every bit of my crazy quilt life," Auntie said as she stitched another colorful piece to the quilt.

Your Turn

1. What was Auntie's advice? Why would this advice be helpful?

_____

_____

2. If a friend needed some advice, what would you tell him or her about God's Word?

_____

_____

Prayer

Lord Jesus, thank You for Your Word. Amen.

 Bodacious Bible Riddles

Paul told his young friend Timothy that knowing what the Bible says would make him wise about being saved by Jesus. That is true for you, too. How well do you know your Bible?

The Bible is made up of two parts: the Old Testament and the New Testament. Each part is made up of books, and each book has a name. Read the riddles and answer the questions. (Use the table of contents in the front of your Bible for help.)

1. I'm the book in the middle of the Bible. I have songs, poems and hymns. Which book am I? (Hint: I'm right before Proverbs.)

   __ __ __ __ __ __

2. I'm the book of beginnings in the front of the Bible.

   __ __ __ __ __ __ __

3. We are the only two books in the Bible with women's names.

   __ __ __ __ and __ __ __ __ __ __

4. We are the four gospels. We tell about the birth, ministry, death and resurrection   of Jesus.

   __ __ __ __ __ __ __, __ __ __ __, __ __ __ __,

   and __ __ __ __

5. I tell about Jesus' return on the last day and about heaven. (Hint: I'm the last book in the Bible.)

   __ __ __ __ __ __ __ __ __ __

The solution is on page 238.

Wisdom

It is wise to ask God for help.

If any of you lacks wisdom, he should ask God, who gives generously to all without finding fault, and it will be given to him.

~ James 1:5

What to Do?

Abbi was working on a poster for art class. At least that's what she had intended to do. But she actually was staring off into space, with a frown creasing her forehead. That's how her dad found her when he came home from work.

"Hi, Princess," he said. "Something wrong?"

"I just don't know what to do," Abbi answered.

Mr. Diem moved around the table and looked at Abbi's poster. "Looks good to me," he said. "You're a good artist. All you need to do is finish it."

Abbi shook her head and said, "I wasn't talking about the poster. I just don't know the right thing to do sometimes when things come up at school. Like when some girls make fun of another girl or something. It's hard to figure out."

"You can always ask God to help you know what to do. Knowing to ask God for help is the beginning of wisdom," Mr. Diem said. "Just like you might ask for my help with this poster. Would that be smart?"

"Hmm. Maybe not," said Abbi with a grin.

Your Turn

1. When you're not sure what to do about a problem, where do you go for advice?

_____

_____

2. Does wisdom mean the same as being smart? Why or why not?

_____

_____

Prayer

Lord, help me to remember to ask for Your help when I'm not sure what to do. Amen.

The Way to Wisdom

The letters (and numbers) below the empty boxes fit in the boxes directly above them, but not necessarily in the order listed. Decide with letter goes in which box and write it in. Cross off each letter as it is used. When your answer is correct, you will have a Bible verse that tells you what can put you on the way to wisdom.

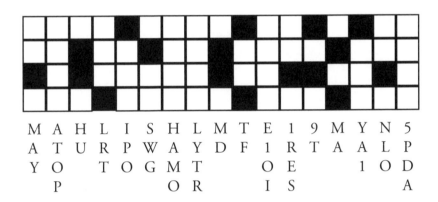

```
M  A  H  L  I  S  H  L  M  T  E  1  9  M  Y  N  5
A  T  U  R  P  W  A  Y  D  F  1  R  T  A  A  L  P
Y  O     T  O  G  M  T     O  E           1  O  D
   P           O  R        I  S              A
```

The solution is on page 238.

Responsible

God wants me to accept responsibility for others.

Each of you should look not only to your own interests,
but also to the interests of others.

~ Philippians 2:4

Nola's Responsibility

"Ooo! Why can't you keep up?" Nola Greene asked.

Garrick had fallen again. Why was he so clumsy? He couldn't seem to walk fast without tripping over something.

Nola tapped her foot while she waited with arms folded. She was so sick of being responsible for her 5-year-old brother! She couldn't even go to the park two blocks from their house without having him tag along.

A small crowd and two police cars near a tall, yellow house caused her to pause. She knew the family that lived in the house. One of them was a girl in her class.

"What's going on?" she asked a boy she knew. He was in a different fifth-grade class.

"Stacey's little sister is missing," he said. "They thought she was out in the backyard playing, but…"

"You should've heard Stacey's mother yelling at her," a girl who stood nearby interrupted. "She was supposed to be watching her. Now nobody knows where she is."

Nola quickly looked down at her little brother. He began to tug on her hand. "Can we go now?" he asked.

Nola nodded. Her little brother was a pain sometimes. But she didn't want anything to happen to him. She held his hand a little tighter.

Your Turn

1. How did Nola feel after learning about Stacey's sister?

_____

_____

2. What are your responsibilities? How do you feel about them?

_____

_____

Prayer

Jesus, thank You for the responsibilities I have. Help me to faithfully carry them out. Amen.

A Walk to the Park

Nola is responsible for taking Garrick to the park. But there are distractions along the way. Help Nola take Garrick to the park and back home again. Distractions to avoid: Nola's friend's house, the ice cream man and friends out skating.

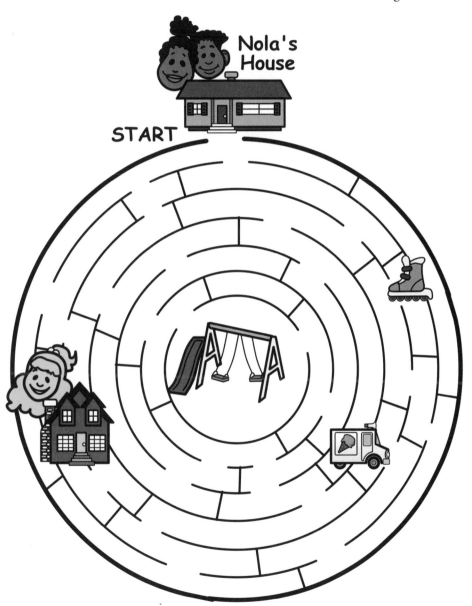

The solution is on page 238.

Responsible

God wants me to take my responsibilities seriously.

Whatever you do, work at it with all your heart,
as working for the Lord, not for men.

~ Colossians 3:23

He's Always Watching

Carmela Wright wrung her hands. "Ow. Hand cramp," she groaned. "I didn't know that stuffing envelopes could be so painful."

"That's 'cause you're trying to be Miss Speedy," Sean said. "You don't have to work so hard. My aunt's way at the front of the store."

Even though Sean's aunt wasn't around, Carmela knew that God was always watching. "Well, I still want to do a good job. It was nice of your aunt to let us do this to make some extra money." Carmela rubbed her hand. "I can't believe I actually got to meet my favorite author and make $25." She stacked the leftover flyers from her pile on top of the flyer-stuffed envelopes.

"Told you I could get you in. It's cool having an aunt who owns a bookstore," said Sean as he sat back in the chair with his arms behind his head.

Carmela noticed how often he had been in that position. He had stuffed one envelope for every five envelopes she had stuffed. His pile of leftover flyers was twice as tall as hers.

Sean's aunt soon appeared. "Well, all done? I see you are, Carmela. Since you've been so dependable, here's a bonus." She handed Carmela an envelope.

Carmela found $20 inside. "Thank you!"

"Sean…"

Sean looked up expectantly.

His aunt put her hand on his shoulder. "I'm afraid you're fired, dear."

Carmela stifled a laugh.

Your Turn

1. What happened as a result?

_____

_____

2. How do you show how seriously you take your responsibilities?

_____

_____

Prayer

God, show me ways to take my responsibilities seriously. Amen.

Responsible for Your Responsibility

Who takes responsibility for helping you be responsible (besides you and your parents)? To find out, color the spaces that have odd numbers.

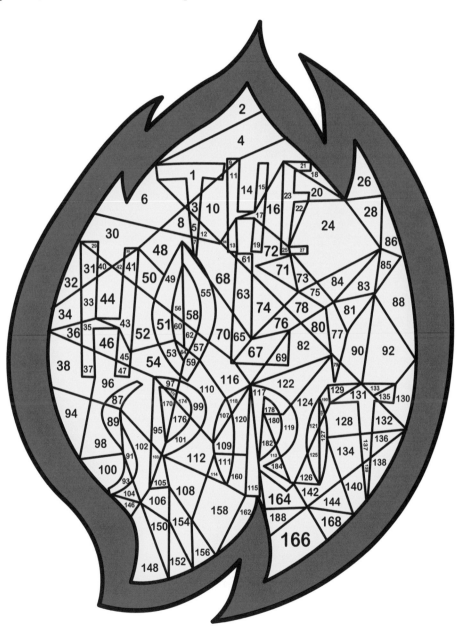

The solution is on page 238.

Responsible

I should value my responsibilities.

*We work hard with our own hands. When we are cursed, we bless;
when we are persecuted, we endure it.*

~ 1 Corinthians 4:12

What's So Great About Responsibility?

"You've got chores? Your parents treat you like a slave!"

Daisy Johnson wished she could agree with Sharon's comment. She was almost sorry that she had said anything to Sharon.

"My parents want me to be responsible, I guess," she mumbled.

Daisy glanced with envy at Sharon's laughing face as they rode the school bus to school. Sharon didn't have to do chores. Her parents gave her lots of spending money. Daisy wished her life could be like that.

As soon as they walked into class, their teacher, Mrs. Nguyen, whispered to Daisy, "I want to talk to you after class."

Daisy stomach flip-flopped. *Now what?* she thought.

"Daisy, I know you're a hardworking, responsible student," Mrs. Nguyen said. "That's why I wanted to recommend you to be on the sixth-grade student council. Each teacher can nominate two students. I'd like to nominate you."

Daisy grinned. *Maybe responsibility isn't so bad!* she thought as she headed off to lunch.

Your Turn

1. Why did Daisy want to be like Sharon?

_____

_____

2. How did Mrs. Nguyen's praise help Daisy?

_____

_____

3. Why do you think being a responsible person is important?

_____

_____

Prayer

Lord, show me how to value responsibility. Amen.

Responsible Drivers?

You know that cars had not been invented during Bible times. But just for fun, which responsible Bible times people would have these license plates? Match the plates with the names in the Name Bank.

The solution is on page 238.

Name Bank

David (1 Samuel 17)

Esther (Esther 1–2)

Joshua (Joshua 6)

Noah (Genesis 6–8)

Ruth (Ruth 1:16-18)

207

Humble

I am humble when I do not consider myself better than others.

In humility consider others better than yourselves.

~ Philippians 2:3

Mr. Plotz

"Hi, Mr. Plotz," Sara O'Hara called to an older man who stacked books on the bookshelf nearest her.

"Hi, girls." He waved, then went back to stacking books.

"Why do you speak to him?" her friend Benita said. She acted as if she wanted to ignore Mr. Plotz.

"He's nice. And always helpful," said Sara.

Benita grabbed her arm. "Come on, there's some space left over here."

They joined the crowd already gathered for a book signing by their favorite new author: E. Arthur Smith. Many of the kids their age seemed to like this author who had written a popular new series.

Soon, one of the bookstore employees came to the microphone to introduce the author. After a round of applause, Sara was stunned to see Mr. Plotz walk forward.

"Hi. I'm sure I caught a lot of you by surprise," Mr. Plotz said. "My pen name is E. Arthur Smith. As many of you know, I've been working in this bookstore for many years. God blessed me to sell a series to a publisher. I've continued working here because I like helping people. Besides, it keeps me humble. After all, if you hadn't liked the series, I wouldn't be standing here today!"

Sara glanced at Benita and almost laughed at the look on her face.

Your Turn

1. How would you expect someone famous to act?

_____

_____

2. Why is humility a valuable quality to have?

_____

_____

Prayer

Help me to be humble, God, as Jesus is. Amen.

Calling on God

Jesus once told a story of two men: a Pharisee and a tax collector. Both went to the temple to pray. But only one man was forgiven. Read about them in Luke 18:9-14, then answer the questions below.

Pharisee   ### Tax Collector

Which man was proud?

_____

Which man was forgiven? Why?

_____

_____

Which man are you like when you pray? Why?

_____

_____

Humble

God wants me to react with humility instead of pride.

*For whoever exalts himself will be humbled, and
whoever humbles himself will be exalted.*

~ Matthew 23:12

The Contest

"Second place!" Stella Neill grumbled as she looked at the ribbon attached to her drawing. "I know my poster's better than this!" She jerked her thumb at the poster next to hers. A large first-place ribbon dangled from it.

"Well, I'm happy with fifth place," her best friend, Iris, said. "I didn't think I'd get a ribbon at all. There are so many cool posters in the contest."

"Most of them are ugly," Stella said. "I worked hard on this school spirit poster. I know I deserve better than second place."

"Sssh. Ms. Watson'll hear you."

Ms. Watson was one of the teachers judging the contest, which took place in the school's gym. She suddenly headed their way. "Oh, girls, there's been a mix-up," she said. "Someone placed the ribbons on the wrong posters. I'm really sorry about this."

Stella threw Iris an I-told-you-so look.

Ms. Watson switched the ribbons around. "There! Now, that's correct."

Stella was stunned to see the fifth-place ribbon hanging from her poster and the first-place ribbon hanging from Iris's poster.

"Congratulations," Ms. Watson said. "Sorry about the mix-up."

Stella made a small noise of rage.

Your Turn

1. Who was humble?

_____

_____

2. When it comes to what you do best, are you like Stella or like Iris? Would someone else say the same thing about you? Why or why not?

_____

_____

Prayer

Lord, You're the one who gave me my abilities. Thank You for what I can do. I also thank You for keeping me humble. Amen.

Your Way to Be Humble

Use your own words (or pictures) to describe what being humble means to you. You might also thank God for what you can do. That's the best way to be humble!

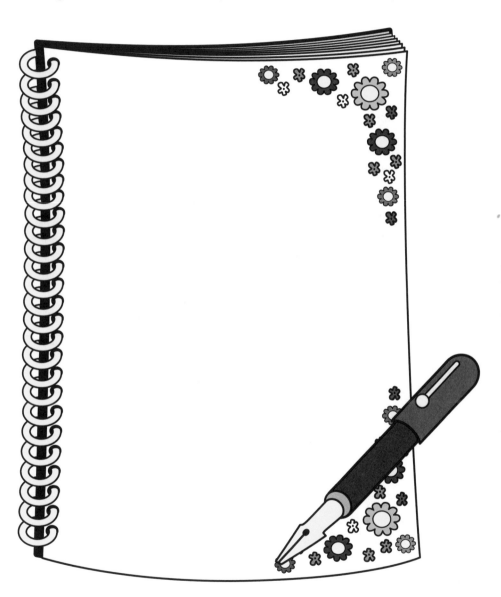

Humble

Humility means putting God first.

Humble yourselves before the Lord, and he will lift you up.

~ James 4:10

Put God First

The kids in Keianna Powers' fifth-grade Sunday school class were filled with questions one particular Sunday. Keianna was the one who had started it all with her question about humility. Why was it important to have? She sat there grinning as others began asking questions.

"Why do we have to ask God for stuff? Why can't He just give us stuff automatically?" Curtis asked.

"Asking Him reminds us that He's God and that we should obey Him," Peter, the college guy who led the class, said. "We're supposed to put Him first. Doing that keeps us humble."

Some of the kids sighed loudly when Peter said the word "humble."

Peter smiled. "That's why we bow our heads when we pray. Some people in the Bible got on their knees and put their faces on the floor. That was a sign of respect."

Peter suddenly dropped to his knees and placed his forehead against the floor. Some of the kids giggled at the sight of him. After a second or two, he got up.

"Wanna try it?" he asked.

No one moved. Peter laughed. "Well, there are other ways of being humble before God. If you're willing to do what He says, then that means you're willing to put Him first."

Your Turn

1. Why do you think being humble before God will cause him to "lift you up"?

_____

_____

2. How do you put God first?

_____

_____

Prayer

When it comes to You, God, help me to have a "You-first" attitude. Amen.

David's Plea

David tried to put God first in all that he did. To read David's words from Psalm 63:1, put the letters below each column in the boxes above that column. The letters may not be listed in the exact order in which they appear in the quote. Mark off used letters at the bottom. A letter may only be used once. The black boxes stand for the end of a word.

The solution is on page 238.

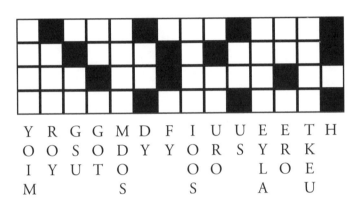

```
Y  R  G  G  M  D  F  I  U  U  E  E  T  H
O  O  S  O  D  Y  Y  O  R  S  Y  R  K
I  Y  U  T  O        O  O        L  O  E
M        S        S        A        U
```

213

Purposeful

God gives purpose to whatever I do.

Whatever you do, work at it with all your heart,
as working for the Lord, not for men.

~ Colossians 3:23

The "To-do" List

The refrigerator door in the Gomez household served as the family bulletin board. There were reminders of appointments and meetings, notices from school, pictures and artwork. The items were constantly changing—except for one thing: Mrs. Gomez's "to-do" list was always on the top left corner.

"Why do you always have that list on the fridge?" Estrella asked her mother.

"Well, it helps keep me focused on what I need to do. It gives me a purpose in my everyday life," her mother explained.

"Do you always get everything done?"

Mrs. Gomez laughed. "Not usually. Then I add them to next week's list or I decide they weren't as important as I thought. But the first thing on the list is always the same."

Estrella read "Work for God" across the top of her mom's list. "What does that mean?" she asked.

"Praying and studying the Bible helps me know what God wants me to do. That gives purpose to my life and work so it's like I'm working for God."

"Hmm, I think I could use a to-do list," decided Estrella.

Your Turn

1. Do you have a to-do list of things you need to do each day or week? Are you successful at accomplishing what's on it? Why or why not?

_____

_____

2. If you could only put three or four things on your "to-do" list for life, what would they be?

_____

_____

Prayer

Lord, help me to focus on You and Your purpose for my life. Amen.

Things To Do

If Bible time people had made "to-do" lists, there would have been some very unusual things on them! Match the person with his or her to-do list by drawing lines between the ones that go together.

David

Noah

Gideon

Small Boy

Abraham

Esther

Ruth

Moses

Joshua

The solution is on page 238.

pack a lunch of 2 loaves of bread and 5 fish

find leftover grain in the field for dinner

pack up my household for a long trip to an unknown place

plan a dinner for the king and prime minister

find 5 smooth stones

move 2 million people to a new home

march around Jericho for a week

find 300 torches and clay jars

collect cypress wood and animals

Purposeful

All things are possible with God.

What is impossible with men is possible with God.

~ Luke 18:27

Make-over List

Madeline and her friend, Quinn, were watching the New Year's Day parade on TV. The girls were giggling and talking about their New Year's Eve sleepover.

In between munching on nachos, pretzels and chips, they "oohed" and "aahed" over the gorgeous floats. During a quiet minute, Madeline heard the TV announcers talking about their New Year's resolutions.

"What's a resolution?" she asked Quinn. Quinn just shrugged her shoulders and kept munching.

Madeline's mom heard her question and answered, "A resolution is when you decide you're going to do something or change something about yourself. On New Year's Day lots of people resolve to do things better in the new year."

Quinn and Madeline decided to make some New Year's resolutions, and soon they were writing like crazy. After a few minutes, Madeline tossed down her paper. "I'd like to change things about myself, but I don't know if I can do these things," she sighed.

"You probably can't do them all by yourself," agreed her mom. "But God can do anything and He can help you keep your resolutions, too."

"Hope I don't keep Him too busy," laughed Madeline as she showed her long list to Quinn.

Your Turn

1. What would you like to change in the way you act or the things you do?

_____

_____

2. How can God help you keep your resolutions?

_____

_____

Prayer

Dear God, help me to change things in my life that need changing. Amen.

I Resolve to...

It doesn't need to be New Year's Day to make resolutions. You can start changing things about yourself any day of the year. Think carefully and be very honest with yourself as you answer these questions.

What are some things about your life, actions and attitudes that need changing?

_____

_____

Pick one of the things from above and make a plan–a resolution–about how to do it. Write your plan here. Is praying to God for help at the top of the list?

_____

_____

Keep track of how you're doing for a month by using this chart.

	Always do it	Sometimes	Hardly Ever
Week 1			
Week 2			
Week 3			
Week 4			

Patient

Waiting takes lots of patience.

A man's wisdom gives him patience.

~ Proverbs 19:11

The Waiting Game

Celia Bailey's mother loved gardening. Each year she had a large vegetable garden crowded with lots of different plants. She also tended flowerbeds filled with gorgeous colors and wonderful smells.

By April, Mrs. Bailey was busy preparing the garden for planting.

"Could I have part of the garden for myself?" Celia asked one year. "And can I plant whatever I want–both vegetables and flowers?"

"That would be great," said her mother. "You can go to the nursery with me and pick out your plants and seeds."

Celia planted a tomato plant and some carrots, no broccoli! She also planted five rows of flower seeds. She watered and weeded and waited. Then she waited some more.

After a week and a half, Celia complained to her mom. "I think the flower seeds were no good. Or maybe the birds ate them. Nothing's coming up and the vegetable plants aren't growing much either."

Her mother laughed. "One thing a gardener needs is lots of patience. Your seeds are fine, they just take a while to sprout–give them another week. But all your patience will pay off when you eat delicious tomatoes and make beautiful bouquets."

Your Turn

1. Do you like waiting for things to happen? Why or why not? How do you handle the waiting?

_____

_____

2. Why is patience an important value?

_____

_____

Prayer

God, sometimes I need lots of patience while I wait for something. Please help me to be patient. Amen.

Avocado Tree

If you're like Celia, you don't have much patience for gardening. So here's a plant that doesn't require much patience: an avocado. You can plant this in the winter during the cold months and it will give you a bit of indoor gardening until you can do the real thing in the spring.

What You Need

avocado seed
sharp nail
three round toothpicks
large glass

What to Do

1. Pierce the avocado seed with a nail to make three holes evenly-spaced around the middle of the seed.

2. Insert a toothpick in each hole.

3. Fill a glass with water and balance the avocado seed on the top, making sure the bottom of the seed is in the water. Check the water often so the bottom of the seed is always covered.

4. Place the glass in front of a window.

5. Soon the seed will begin to produce a shoot and a root. As soon as the shoot has a few leaves, snip off the top leaves to encourage the plant to branch out.

6. Pot the little tree when the roots are thick. If you live in a place where it never freezes, you can plant the tree outside. Remember to keep it watered.

7. You can do the same thing with a sweet potato, but don't snip off the leaves. The sweet potato will make a beautiful green vine!

Patient

Making something beautiful takes patience.

But if we hope for what we do not yet have, we wait for it patiently.

~ Romans 8:25

Tangled Threads

Aunt Sally was helping Carmen stitch a sampler for her mom's birthday. She showed Carmen how to read the directions and make some of the stitches. It looked easy enough.

But when Carmen tried doing it on her own, it didn't seem quite so easy. After two hours, it looked as though she had hardly done anything!

This is taking too long, Carmen thought. *I'll take some shortcuts. I don't need to follow all these directions.*

"How's it going?" Aunt Sally asked later as she came into the room.

"Not so good," mumbled Carmen. "I worked all morning and hardly anything is done. And I have a big lump of tangled threads on the back."

Aunt Sally asked, "Did you follow the directions, step by step?"

"Well, most of them," Carmen said.

"You have to work very carefully and follow every direction when you do stitchery," said Aunt Sally. "When you hurry and skip some directions, you end up with a big mess."

"It takes so long to do all that sorting and counting," Carmen said.

"To sew a beautiful sampler, you need to be very patient. It's not something that's done in one day. When it's finally finished, you can really be proud of it," said Aunt Sally.

This will be a sewing masterpiece, even if it takes all summer, thought Carmen as she carefully snipped the tangled threads and started over.

Your Turn

1. When do you become impatient?

_____

_____

2. What are some of the things that can happen when you're impatient?

_____

_____

Prayer

Thanks for being patient with me. Help me to learn to be more patient. Amen.

Patience of Job

A believer from the Old Testament, Job is often called a patient man. When everything in his life went wrong, he wanted to talk to God. Instead, God asked Job some questions to help him understand that God takes care of everything in His time. Fill in the blanks, using verses from Job 39 in an NIV Bible. The answers are on page 238.

Do you know when the mountain _____ give birth?

Who let the wild _____ go free?

Will the wild _____ consent to serve you?

The wings of the _____ flap joyfully, but they cannot compare with the feathers of the

_____.

Do you give the _____ his strength?

Does the _____ take flight by your wisdom?

Does the _____ soar at your command?

Patient

God wants me to be patient with others.

Love is patient, love is kind.

~ 1 Corinthians 13:4

Hurry Up!

Ashley, 12, and Delaney, 6, were spending the weekend with Aunt Gloria at her farm. Yesterday had been wonderful–especially riding the horses. But today was gray, cold and rainy. Ashley was tired of reading. She was quickly getting bored.

"Next Sunday is Father's Day. Do you have stuff to make a poster or a card for Dad?" Ashley asked her aunt.

"You bet! I never throw away anything and I have a bunch of stuff left from the art course I taught," Aunt Gloria answered as she showed them her supplies.

"Wow!" exclaimed Delaney as she looked around. "Just like an art store!"

The girls decided to make a giant poster card. They soon had all the materials on the table. Ashley lettered "Happy Father's Day" in big capital letters. Then she colored in "Happy" with markers. Delaney worked on "Father's."

"Hurry up, I can't do the next word until you finish," said Ashley.

Ashley drew a horse and then impatiently waited for Delaney to draw grass and flowers. "Oh, let me do it! You're taking too long," she yelled at Delaney.

"Forget it! I quit," cried Delaney and threw down her marker.

"Whoa! Hold your horses!" said Aunt Gloria. "What's the rush, Ashley? Looks like it's going to rain all day. Remember that Delaney is six years younger than you. She can't do things as fast as you. You need to be patient."

Ashley knew Aunt Gloria was right. She gave Delaney a hug and said, "I'm sorry I was such a boss. Fill that field with flowers and grass. Take as long as you want."

"This horse will have so much to eat, he'll get fat!" laughed Delaney as she grabbed the green marker.

Your Turn

1. What do you do when you lose your patience?

_____

_____

2. Why is it wrong to lose your patience?

_____

_____

Prayer

Lord, help me to be more patient with people and things that concern me. Amen.

Give Me Patience!

Are you more patient with some people than with others? Check your patience level with each person listed below. You may need patience to do this activity!

	LOTS	SOME	LITTLE	NONE
Waiting for your mom to take you to the mall.				
Listening to your uncle tell the same joke for the third time.				
Helping your little sister learn to ride her bike.				
Having your big brother tell you how to do something.				
Taking a walk with your grandpa, who uses a cane.				
Helping a friend with homework.				
Listening to your teacher explain something you already know.				
Waiting for a neighbor to pay you for babysitting.				
Doing drills for the coach during practice.				
Being in a checkout line with a very slow cashier.				
Giving directions to a stranger.				

Initiating

I can use initiative by doing something without being asked.

For Titus not only welcomed our appeal, but he is coming to you with much enthusiasm and on his own initiative.

~ 2 Corinthians 8:17

Everybody or Nobody?

Kelia and Sam were surprised to see their dad when they came in the back door.

"Hey, Dad, you're home early," Kelia said as she shrugged out of her backpack and dropped it in the corner. Her jacket landed on top of it.

"What's up?" asked Sam in a muffled voice. His head was stuck inside the refrigerator looking for something to eat. "There sure isn't much food in here."

"I'm home early because I'm picking up your mom at the airport in an hour," said Dad. "Her meeting finished early, so she's coming home today instead of tomorrow. I'm not sure she'll be happy about the way things look around here."

"I thought Kelia would pick up," Sam said as he looked at the disorder.

"Oh, sure," Kelia shot back. "And I thought you would get some food."

Dad cleared his throat. "Let me tell you a story," he said. "The Body family complained about the trash and junk littering the neighborhood. Every Body thought it looked terrible. He said Some Body should clean it up. Any Body could do it! Every Body thought Some Body would do the job. So No Body did it."

Kelia and Sam got the message and started cleaning by putting away their school things.

"Drive slow to give us some time!" said Kelia as Dad went out the door.

Your Turn

1. How can your initiating action help others?

_____

_____

2. How can others by affected when you don't initiate needed action?

_____

Prayer

Lord, help me to notice what needs doing and then take action. Amen.

Surprise Salad

Take the initiative and surprise your family with this yummy salad. It is actually delicious enough to be eaten as a dessert!

What You Need

1 cup of Mandarin oranges

1 cup of crushed pineapple

1 cup of miniature marshmallows

1 cup of coconut

1 cup of sour cream

What to Do

1. Find a bowl large enough to hold all the ingredients.

2. Drain the juice off of the oranges and the pineapple.

3. Put the oranges, pineapple, marshmallows and coconut into the bowl.

4. Pour the cup of sour cream over the top. Stir all the ingredients together until they are well mixed.

5. Refrigerate for half an hour.

6. Enjoy!

Initiating

I should use initiative to talk to others about God.

*Ask and it will be given to you; seek and you will find;
knock and the door will be opened to you.*

~ Matthew 7:7

Inviting Rachel

Ellie and Rachel were in fifth grade together. Ellie had been in Wilder Elementary School since kindergarten. Rachel was a new student at the beginning of the school year. Ellie liked Rachel, and by the time Christmas rolled around they had become friends.

"I don't know if Rachel knows about Jesus," Ellie said to her mother. "We were talking about Christmas and she never mentioned going to church or anything. I wish she could come to our church sometime."

"Maybe you could initiate it," answered her mom.

Ellie had a puzzled look on her face. "Initiate–I don't know what that word means."

"Sorry," laughed Mom. "I guess that is an adult word. It means to see that something needs to be done and then doing it without being told. In plain language, why don't you ask Rachel to come to a Christmas service with you?"

"Hey, thanks, Mom. Think I'll initiate a phone call to Rachel right now."

Your Turn

1. Why was it important for Ellie to have initiative?

_____

_____

2. Think about people and things in your church, school or family. Can you have initiative and take some needed action? Why or why not?

_____

_____

Prayer

Jesus, sometimes it's hard to have initiative. Help me take action when I see something needs to be done. Amen.

Taking Action

You can read about Bible people who took action when something needed to be done. Look up the Bible passages below and write the name of the person on the lines. When you have filled in all the names, put the circled letters on the matching numbered lines to discover an important value that all of them shared.

The solution is on page 238.

He took action as a soldier (1 Samuel 14:1, 6-7)

— — — — ◯ — — —
　　　　　4, 7

He wanted to build a house of worship (2 Samuel 7:1-5) — — ◯◯ ◯
　　　　　　　　　9　5, 8

He wanted to repair the crumbling temple (2 Chronicles 24:4, 5)

— — ◯ — —
　　　6

She wanted healing from Jesus (Matthew 9:19-22) — — — — ◯
　　　　　　　　　　　　　　2

He had questions for Jesus (John 3:1, 2)

— ◯ — — — ◯ — — —
　1, 3　　　　10

All of these people had — — — — — — — — — —.
　　　　　　　　　1　2　3　4　5　6　7　8　9　10

Trustworthy

True friends can be trusted.

A gossip betrays a confidence, but a trustworthy man keeps a secret.

~ Proverbs 11:13

Please Don't Tell!

Shaleena and Kylie had been friends since kindergarten. They spent a lot of time at each other's homes doing homework, playing or just hanging out.

But lately Kylie noticed a change in Shaleena. She didn't ask Kylie to come to her house very often and she didn't joke around or laugh as much as she usually did.

"Let's go to your house and do our math homework," Kylie suggested one day as they walked home from school.

"Oh, well, I don't think so," stammered Shaleena. "I, uh, have to do something."

"Are you mad at me?" Kylie asked. "You never want me to come to your house. If you don't want to be my friend anymore, just tell me."

Shaleena started to cry. "I'm not mad at you and I do want to be your friend, but I'm scared and worried. My dad lost his job a month ago and can't find another one. There isn't much money and then my mom and dad fight and yell. That's why I didn't want you to come over. Please don't tell anyone!"

The next day at lunch, Cassie sat next to Kylie. "What's with Shaleena?" she asked. "She doesn't seem to want to be friends with anyone. She hardly talks to us and just wants to be by herself. Guess she just thinks she's too good for us."

Your Turn

1. If you were Kylie, how would you answer Cassie? Have you ever been in that kind of a situation? What did you do?

_____

_____

2. Can others trust you not to tell their secrets or gossip?

_____

_____

Prayer

Dear God, help me to be a trustworthy friend and not gossip about others. Amen.

🌸 Wanted: A Good Friend 🦋

If you could advertise for a good friend in the newspaper or on the Internet, for what would you ask? Check off what you would list.

❏ smart

❏ athletic

❏ trustworthy

❏ neat clothes

❏ Christian

❏ loving

❏ wealthy

❏ lets me copy her homework

❏ part of the popular crowd

❏ sticks up for me

❏ sense of humor

❏ goes along with others

❏ prays and studies the Bible

❏ helpful

❏ patient

Which of the words above describe your qualifications as a friend?

_____

_____

Trustworthy

I should be trustworthy in all I do.

Whoever can be trusted with very little can also be trusted with much.

~ Luke 16:10

New Year, New Job

Tara was part of the Rainbow Club at church. The Rainbow Club was for girls in grades 5 to 7. They met every other week for Bible study, crafts, games and other fun things. Tara had made lots of friends at the club and always looked forward to going.

Last year when Tara was in sixth grade, Miss Paulson had asked her to be the snack chairman. That meant that Tara had to ask someone to bring snacks each time. She kept a list to be sure everyone had a turn.

Now Tara was in seventh grade and it was her last year in the Rainbow Club. Before the first meeting, Miss Paulson talked to Tara after church. "I would like you to be in charge of the crafts and games this year," she said. "It's a big job and you will need to have some other girls help you. Will you do it?"

Tara was flattered to be asked. She knew it was the most important job in the whole club. "Thanks for asking me. I'd love to do it if you think I can handle it," she answered.

Miss Paulson gave her a quick hug. "Great, Tara! I know you can do it just fine. You're very trustworthy. I never even thought about snacks last year because I knew you would take care of it. You proved that you are organized and take your responsibilities seriously. Thanks for saying yes."

On the way home, Tara started thinking about some fun crafts and crazy games to play. It would be a great year!

Your Turn

1. Can people depend on your help even when it may mean a lot of work or may be inconvenient for you? Why or why not?

_____

_____

2. Why is it important to be trustworthy?

_____

_____

Prayer

Lord, help me be trustworthy in small things as well as big ones. Amen.

Look Closely

Look at this!

What do you see? Turn the page to the right (clockwise). Now what do you see? Do you see the rabbit or the duck more easily?

Study this picture!

What do you see? Look again. Can you see something different? Do you see a vase or two people facing each other?

How about you?

What do people see when they look at you? Do they see a reliable, trustworthy girl who will do what she promises? Write a description of yourself–not how you look but how you act and speak. Would you want yourself for a best friend?

_____

_____

_____

Puzzle Answers

page 23

					J	O	H	N
					O			
		D	A	N	I	E	L	
					A		O	
					T		T	
J	O	S	E	P	H			
	E			A		P		
	S			N	O	A	H	
R	U	T	H			U		
	S					L		

page 25
God wants us to be loyal to Him and His Word.

page 27

These people repented. You can, too.

page 29
Turn back to God.

page 31
1. JESUS, 2. FAMILY, 3. LOVE, 4. HOME, 5. FRIENDS, 6. FOOD, 7. SCHOOL, 8. COMPUTER, 9. GAMES, 10. CHURCH, 11. ENJOYMENT, 12. CLOTHES, 13. HEAVEN

page 35
Today in the town of David a Savior has been born to you: he is Christ the Lord.

page 37
I WILL PUT YOU IN CHARGE OF MANY THINGS. (Matthew 25:23)

page 41
The <u>Helper</u>, the <u>Holy</u> <u>Spirit</u>, will <u>teach</u> you everything.

page 43
Follow His commands.
Obey my parents.
Tell others the Good News.

page 45
I am the first and I am the last; apart from me there is no God.

page 47

page 55

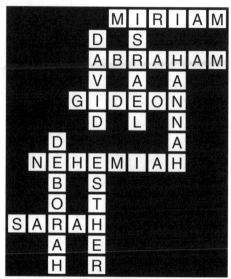

page 57

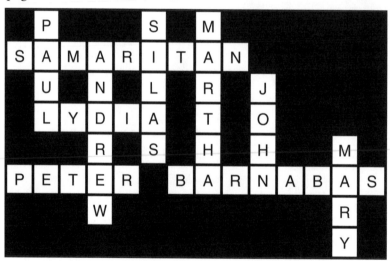

page 65
May it be to me as you have said.

page 67
Jesus has your best interests at heart.

page 71
SINNERS, TAX COLLECTORS,
BLIND, LAME, POOR, LEPERS,
CHILDREN, BEGGARS

page 77
1. i, 2. h, 3. e, 4. g, 5. f, 6. j, 7. k,
8. a, 9. d, 10. c, 11. l, 12. b

page 83

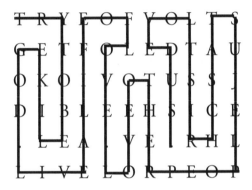

Try to be like God. Live a life of
love. Love other people just as
Christ loved us. (Ephesians 5:1-2)

page 85
Be devoted to one another in
brotherly love. Honor one another
above yourselves.

page 87
You'll need a sincere <u>heart</u>.

page 89
SMALL
DOLLAR
GIVE
JESUS
Hidden Answer: LOVE

page 93
1. BARNABAS
2. SAPPHIRA
3. WIDOW
4. PAUL
5. GIVE
The WILLINGNESS to SHARE
with others.

page 95
If you cheat even a little, you won't
be honest with greater responsibilities.

page 97
The Lord detests lying lips, but he
delights in men who are truthful.

page 111
Show mercy and compassion to
one another.

page 113
WE HAVE THE MIND OF
CHRIST.

page 115
Think of others instead of yourself

page 117
chore, pray, love, gentle, time, help

page 125

band, sport teams, Army, church family, orchestra, fire fighters, classmates, home builders

page 127

I appeal to you…that all of you agree with one another. (1 Corinthians 1:10)

page 129

```
S  K  N  A  H  T  W  O  R  D
T  R  J  E  N  A  H  N  D  E
H  E  W  H  A  T  E  V  E  R
R  H  L  T  M  T  T  E  E  A
O  T  L  R  E  L  H  E  D  N
U  A  A  S  U  S  E  J  E  D
G  F  A  G  O  D  R  O  L  L
H  I  M  L  W  U  O  Y  O  W
```

page 131

Father forgive them, for they do not know what they are doing.

page 133

1. As the Lord forgave you.
2. Anyone who sins against you.
3. Because you are forgiven.
4. As often as he asks for forgiveness.

page 137

Make sure that nobody pays back wrong for wrong, but always try to be kind to each other and to everyone else. 1 Thessalonians 5:15

page 139

The Lord will teach you to be kind.

page 141

goodness, knowledge, self-control, perseverance, godliness, brotherly kindness, love

page 145

page 161

A kid is flying a kite with no string, the tree is the wrong type for the beach, there is a phone booth in the middle of the water, one girl has on boots, a fish is sunbathing, the sun has a starfish in it, two people are arguing. The two could stop arguing and make peace with each other.

page 163

THE LORD IS MY STRENGTH AND MY SHIELD. MY HEART RESTS IN HIM AND I AM HELPED.

page 165

God will help you. Just have faith!

page 167

Never <u>will</u> I <u>leave</u> you; <u>never</u> will I <u>forsake</u> you." So we say with <u>confidence</u>, "The Lord is my <u>helper</u>; I will not be <u>afraid</u>. What can man do to <u>me</u>?"

page 169

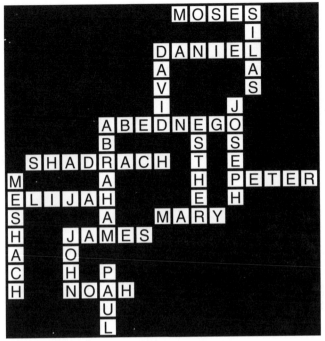

page 171
Trust in the Lord with all your heart. (Proverbs 3:5)

page 173
Blessed is the man who trusts in the Lord, whose confidence is in him. Jeremiah 17:7

page 181
Be joyful in hope, patient in affliction, faithful in prayer. Romans 12:12

page 183
Instead of thinking sad thoughts, rejoice!

page 187
It is by grace you have been saved.

page 193

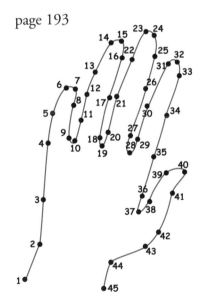

page 195

page 197
Instruct a wise man and he will be wiser still. (Proverbs 9:9)

page 199
1. Psalms, 2. Genesis, 3. Ruth, Esther, 4. Matthew, Mark, Luke, John, 5. Revelation

page 201
Your word is a lamp to my feet and a light to my path.
(Psalm 119:105)

page 203

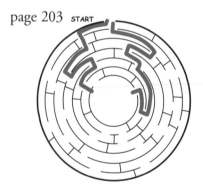

page 205

page 207
2 BY 2 = Noah
U GO I GO = Ruth
GNT KLR = David
BEEUT = Esther
WALL FALL = Joshua

page 213
O GOD YOU ARE MY GOD. I SEEK YOU. MY SOUL THIRSTS FOR YOU.

page 215
David – find 5 small stones; Noah – collect cypress wood and animals; Gideon – find 300 torches and clay jars; Small boy – pack a lunch of 2 loaves of bread and 5 fish; Abraham – pack up my household for a long trip to an unknown place; Esther – plan a dinner for a king and prime minister; Ruth – find leftover grain in the field for dinner; Moses – move 2 million people to a new home; Joshua – march around Jericho for a week

page 221
goats, donkey, ox, ostrich, stork, horse, hawk, eagle

page 227
Jonathan
David
Joash
Woman
Nicodemus
initiative

# My Prayer Reminders

On this page, you can jot down people and needs about which you want to talk to God. When you pray, you can check these pages so you don't forget anything.

My Favorite Verses

Sometimes when you read the Bible, you'll find a verse or a sentence that really touches your heart. Use this page to write down those verses so you can have them handy.